Different Perspectives on the Syrian Reality

Research in the Diverse Fields of Syrian Culture

edited by Ettijahat – Independent Culture

Participating researchers: Alina Oueishek, Hani Al Telfah, Mohammad Omran, Wasim Raif Al Salti

D1453225

DIFFERENT PERSPECTIVES ON THE SYRIAN REALITY

Research in the Diverse Fields of Syrian Culture

edited by Ettijahat – Independent Culture

Participating researchers: Alina Oueishek, Hani Al Telfah, Mohammad Omran, Wasim Raif Al Salti

ibidem-Verlag
Stuttgart

Bibliographic information published by the Deutsche Nationalbibliothek
Die Deutsche Nationalbibliothek lists this publication in the Deutsche Nationalbibliografie;
detailed bibliographic data are available in the Internet at http://dnb.d-nb.de.

Bibliografische Information der Deutschen Nationalbibliothek
Die Deutsche Nationalbibliothek verzeichnet diese Publikation in der Deutschen
Nationalbibliografie; detaillierte bibliografische Daten sind im Internet über http://dnb.d-nb.de
abrufbar.

Proof-reading: The Language Platform, Jad El Hajj
Cover design: Ibrahim Brimo
Photo cover courtesy of Mohamad Khayata, Aegean Sea
Foreword by Hassan Abbas, Phd.

Ettijahat-Independent Culture
Main office: Boulevard Louis Schmidt 119, box 3,1040,
Etterbeek, Belgique
Regional office: Younes Gebeili Street, Hanna bldg 30, Mar Mikhael,
Beirut, Lebanon.
Phone: 00961-1-442770
Email: info@ettijahat.org
Website: www.ettijahat.org

Opinions explained within these research papers do not necessarily reflect Ettijahat's opinion
nor its members.

ISBN-13: 978-3-8382-1161-9

© *ibidem*-Verlag / *ibidem* Press
Stuttgart, Germany 2018

Printed in the United States of America

Research:
To Strengthen the Culture of Knowledge

This capacity-building programme aims to provide an opportunity for full-time commitment for Syrian and Palestinian-Syrian young researchers (22–40 years old) to explore the field of cultural studies. The programme seeks to enhance their research skills, guide them and enable them to accomplish their research project (the programme will most likely be their first such venture following their academic studies). Experienced cultural researchers, who are part of the Selection Committee for the programme, will directly supervise these projects.

The current edition of the programme's annual course consists of three key phases:

1) Application submission and selection of young researchers
2) Training and skill enhancement
3) Completion of actual research, supervised by experienced researchers.

The programme will focus on current trends in cultural research which are relevant to the situation in Syria, especially changes in the perspectives of Syrian artists with regard to their relationship with society and the transformations it is witnessing.

Programme Team

Nada Farah – Programme Manager
Mossaad Assaad – Programme Coordinator

Ettijahat-Independent Culture would like to express its gratitude to all its partners for their support. Special thanks goes to Mimeta – Centre for Culture Sector Development and Arts Cooperation for their support since the beginning of the programme and for their faith in the value of cultural research.

We owe our utmost recognition to all the respectable Trainers, Lecturers, Scientific Committee Members and Mentors, with whom we have had the privilege of collaborating, particularly for their efforts, involvements and commitments. Special mention in this regard is due to Hassan Abbas, PhD, and Marianne Njeim, PhD.

The programme would not have had the same impression were it not for the involvement of the Young Researchers, who have shown genuine enthusiasm and seriousness in conducting research on topics related to their country, communities and fields of work, and from whom we—as a team—have learned a great deal.

Last but not least, we would like to thank Ranya Assassa for her support.

www.ettijahat.org
Facebook: Ettijahat-Independent Culture
Twitter: EttijahatIndep
Youtube: Ettijahat-Independent Culture

HEINRICH
BÖLL
STIFTUNG
MIDDLE EAST

Liberté • Égalité • Fraternité
RÉPUBLIQUE FRANÇAISE

MINISTÈRE
DE L'EUROPE ET DES
AFFAIRES ÉTRANGÈRES

Contents

Children in the Shadow of the Islamic State:

Foreword

Hassan Abbas, PhD.

"The total number of full-time researchers in the Arab countries, including faculty members, is 35,000...[1]" Today, this number has undoubtedly decreased, considering the fact that many researchers have been forced to leave their countries since the publication of this figure in 2003, due to the tragic situation of the Arab world and the demise of its scientific, intellectual and research institutions.

The scientific research scene in the Arab world is not particularly promising. We would not, in my opinion, be mistaken to establish a causal link between this gloomy scene and the level of violence in the region or the underdeveloped discourse prevalent in Arab societies. Science alone is capable of driving nations towards the establishment of societies that promote human dignity, and it is the only guarantor to overcome oppression and to ensure progress and civility. Nations that are institutionally concerned with science and research enjoy the highest degrees of freedom and development. The pioneers of the Arab renaissance became aware of this fact and focused their projects on enhancing science through the establishment of higher institutes and centres for scientific research, as did Muhammad Ali[2] in the first half of the nineteenth century. However, the turbulent history of the region had prevented stability, which is a prerequisite for progressive and pioneering projects to flourish. The history of the region is one of war and uncertainty, much more so than one of peace and stability. Prolonged periods of destruction and demolition are incomparable to the scarce moments of building and urbanisation. Consecutive wars have deprived the region of the privilege of directing its attention towards the establishment of scientific institutions and research centres, and towards nurturing future generations of scientific researchers. While it is true that many Arab countries have created research centres affiliated with state or military institutions, most of these centres spe-

---

[1] Arab Human Development Report 2003, *Towards a Knowledge Society*, UNDP, Arab Fund for Economic and Social Development. P. 72
[2] https://www.britannica.com/biography/Muhammad-Ali-pasha-and-viceroy-of-Egypt

cialise in fields related to the state's authoritarian and security functions, rather than to human development. Continuous wars, especially the Israeli occupation of Arab territories, have forced Arab countries to focus their expenditures on the war effort, which constantly drains a large proportion of their capabilities. Nonetheless, this excuse—which is no doubt legitimate—has turned into a pretext to justify the failure of Arab countries in establishing the real foundations of states that are capable of achieving the aspirations of their citizens in terms of security, development and stability. The most important of these foundations is the consolidation of the research community, primarily through the establishment of scientific research institutions.

States that have failed to perform their duty of establishing scientific research institutions should instead have created favourable conditions for civil society to carry out this task. It is normal for civil society to assume the responsibilities that the state is incapable or unwilling to fulfil. However, the revolutionary regimes that rose to power in their respective countries were not concerned with gaining legitimacy through persuasion and participation as much as they sought to impose and secure their grip on power through repression and domination. In fact, these regimes have restricted freedoms and antagonised civil society and disrupted its energies. Rather than directing their policies towards developing human capital, these regimes have focused on the development of their repressive organs to the point where democracy has become confined to strict security limitations: everything is planned or established from the perspective of security—the security of these regimes, that is. This was, for many years, the general picture of the so-called revolutionary regimes, including the Syrian regime.

Syrian civil society had suffered for decades from these circumstances, until the beginning of the millennium, which brought forth a revival in this field, albeit characterised by the concurrence of two contradictory phenomena: on the one hand, the regime created a civil organisation, which was both a governmental and non-governmental organisation—GoNGO[3]. The regime did not hesitate to support and strengthen this organisation, giving it wide-ranging influence in the field of development and culture. On the other hand, the regime con-

---

[3]   Syrian Trust for Development.

tinued to clamp down on organised civil activities, especially those handling intellectual, cultural and human rights issues. Concurrently, many young Syrians embarked on individual or collective creative activities. Musical bands witnessed a surprising boom, many theatrical companies emerged and presented their work in alternative venues, and cinema clubs attracted a wide young audience, not to mention the establishment of several reading clubs, etc. Amid this atmosphere of independent cultural development, craving freedom and creativity, Ettijahat-Independent Culture was born. It introduces itself as "a cultural organisation that is active in the field of independent culture in Syria and the Arab region. It seeks to activate the role of independent culture and arts in order to play a positive role in the process of cultural, political and social change. It also seeks to contribute to building a genuine relationship between cultural and artistic work on the one hand and Syria's diverse communities on the other hand…"[4]

Ettijahat has defined three main focus areas, namely:

1) To contribute to the revitalisation of the artistic movement, and to cooperate with independent artists and cultural actors;
2) To contribute to the development of cultural policies and the basic trends of culture and arts at the national level;
3) To contribute to the development of field and academic studies and research.

Indeed, after its establishment, *Ettijahat* proceeded to work on projects related to these specific axes. Its first project was a programme to train and support young researchers aged between 22 and 40 years to undertake research in the cultural field. To date, *Ettijahat* has completed four trainings, the first of which was held in Damascus and the remaining three in Beirut. Preparations are underway to launch the fifth edition of the project.

The percentage of participation in these trainings can be more accurately identified through the following detailed table:

---

[4]   Information available on *Ettijahat's* website: www.ettijahat.org.

	Applicants	Trainees	Research Completed	Female / Male	Outside / Inside Syria
First Edition	31	11	11	4/7	1/10
Second Edition	38	14	10	4/6	5/5
Third Edition	40	8	9	4/6	6/4
Fourth Edition	38	9	9	6/3	6/3
Total	147	42	39	18/22	18/22

At the beginning of each edition, researchers engage in an intensive training workshop on the concept of culture, research methodologies and principles of research writing. After that, specialised mentors direct the researchers' work throughout the entire duration of the project. The mentors directly oversee the completion of research papers. Over the past few years, some of these studies were published independently[5]. However, in 2016, *Ettijahat* selected five research papers completed under the second edition of the programme and published them in one book[6]. In the book you now have in your hands, *Ettijahat* presents examples of research papers carried out under its pioneering project. A committee of specialised researchers has carefully chosen the following research papers based on a set of criteria:

1) *Features of the Home in the Refugee Camp-Applied Study on Al Jarahiya Camp*, by Alina Oueishek
2) *Political Stereotypes in the Syrian Uprising*, by Hani Al Telfah.
3) *Imagery of the Tormented Body in Contemporary Syrian Art*, by Mohammad Omran
4) *Children in the Shadow of the Islamic State*: *Jihadi Schooling and Recruitment*, by Wasim Raif Al Salti

These research papers, and the majority of studies completed, are characterised by the seriousness of the topics and a clear commitment to academic rigor and research ethics, which will be clearly evident to those interested in reading this book.

---

[5]   See, for example: Alia Ahmed, *The Reality of Syrian Women in the Current Crisis*, Citizen House Publishing (Syrian League for Citizenship), Damascus, 2014.

[6]   *Research: to Strengthen the Culture of Knowledge—Five Research Papers on Contemporary Syrian Questions*, Mamdouh Adwan Publishing House, 2016.

The initiative taken by *Ettijahat* to train researchers and encourage them to explore various cultural domains deserves our admiration and encouragement for several reasons, notably:

1) It provides a successful model for what can be accomplished by civil society in the field of research and scientific progress;
2) It provides a successful model for what can be accomplished by localising research as a necessary step for building a national research community;
3) It contributes to establishing a research movement that relies on active young people and liberates their abilities;
4) It contributes to investigating Syrian society by focusing research on different contexts of the current Syrian reality;
5) It contributes to strengthening citizenship by allowing young researchers to work on the issues they face in life.

The Syrian crisis has attracted the attention of research centres in many countries and has aroused the interest of many governmental and non-governmental organisations. Researchers of all stripes have come to work on topics related to Syria, and this fact cannot be ignored and should not be criticised or rejected under any pretext. Rather, we ought to praise and celebrate the national initiatives taken to understand, study and analyse the issues of Syrian society. Such efforts are at the core of *Ettijahat's* work, of which we find an exquisite representation in this book.

Features of the Home in the Refugee Camp

Applied Study on Al Jarahiya Camp

Prepared by: Alina Oueishek
Supervised by: Omar Abdulaziz Al Hallaj
Research conducted in 2014–2015

Acknowledgment

I would like to thank my research supervisor, Mr. Omar Abdulaziz Al Hallaj, who has helped me a great deal with his guidance throughout all the different stages of this work and put me back on the right track whenever I lost focus.

My heartfelt love and appreciation go to Sabah Al Hallak and Hassan Abbas, without whom this research would have never seen the light of day. I thank them for their presence and unwavering support, as well as for their trust in this work and my ability to accomplish it.

Dad: now that the research is published, my deepest gratitude and love go to you.

Summary

Although the camp may appear as one whole entity for an outsider, in terms of areas and spaces, it is in fact divided into separate communities by a series of invisible delimitations drawn by the social roles and relationships that exist among refugees. Men and children dominate open public spaces, and men specifically can be seen ambulating around the camp during the day without any restriction on their movement. By contrast, the lives of women are more severely affected by those invisible delimitations, as the constraints they impose on women's mobility between tents also reflect their family traditions.

This research paper examines the architectural environment of Al Jarahiya refugee camp in Lebanon's Bekaa Valley, including the way in which the refugees have shaped this camp and the physical and invisible borders they have established within it, in order to understand the various relationships that influence and are influenced by the surrounding architectural environment.

The paper also tackles the various levels of the camp's composition: the general borders of the tents and their environment; clusters formed by a number of neighboring or adjacent tents or by a tent that houses more than one family; and the relationships and space distribution inside a single tent. All of these factors are considered in light of the radius of mobility and the visible and invisible boundaries set for both women and children, as well and the mechanisms by which these boundaries are set.

The paper mainly focuses on the reciprocal relationships that emerge between housing units and the communities established within them, looking at both individuals and groups and how their relationships affect the delimitation of visible and invisible borders, particularly for women and children. To analyse this aspect of life in the camp, a series of pivotal questions must be answered in order to address the main research question: what are the vital spaces that constitute Al Jarahiya camp? What are the types of housing and activities that exist in it? What forms do the clusters in the camp take? Why are these clusters shaped the way they are? What are the visible and invisible boundaries governing the movements and gatherings of the camp's residents? How are they defined? How do these boundaries affect the participation of women and children in public life?

The paper is based on the general assumption that there is an inevitable dialectic relationship between housing and culture, which affects the way housing units are built and organised and forges the relationships among the individuals living within the same housing unit, as well as the relationship that these individuals have with their neighborhood. The way in which the camp's housing units are structured also becomes a significant factor that influences the cultural lifestyle of the people living there.

The research paper also seeks to understand the different relationships created in the camp, which influence or are influenced by the surrounding architectural environment, through a scientific examination of models that were recorded during field visits. The paper also documents the effects of displacement as an emergency situation widely affecting the relationships and lifestyles within Syrian society, in addition to causing a humanitarian crisis in neighboring countries, particularly in Lebanon. In the conclusion, the paper offers a series of recommendations for relevant institutions and for actors within camps.

The researcher starts by giving a general description of the situation that has led to the displacement of Syrians and the establishment of the analysed camp, by presenting a glimpse of the armed conflict in Syria which has generated this new social environment (the refugee camp). She also provides some information on the origins of Al Jarahiya camp as an empirical model for the study of the camp's physical environment and the interactions of refugees with it.

The paper then describes the architectural environment of the tents and their formation, as well as how they interact with each other and with their surroundings, by illustrating the camp layout on three levels (the tent, the cluster and the camp with its periphery). In order to analyse these three levels, the research methodology relies on case studies and samples of families and individuals living in the camp. It also adopts a descriptive approach in order to analyse specific examples of the camp's architectural spaces (tents, clusters, markets, roads, etc.), to identify the people who form and occupy these spaces and to describe how they interact with each other and with their surroundings. This aims at understanding the reciprocal and dialectic relationship between the refugees' culture and their new dwellings, as well as to detect the changes that their new type of settlement has imposed on their lifestyle.

In her analysis of the first level (the tent), the researcher has relied on two models: the first model is a tent where a family of three brothers and their sister live, while the second model consists of two related families living in the same tent: a woman with her husband and six children and her sister – a long-time divorcee – with her two daughters. This part thoroughly describes the nature of the tents and the interior and exterior spaces that define them, along with the visible and invisible borders that constrict the mobility of the tenants and their daily activities, with special focus on women and children.

In the part focusing on the second level, the researcher describes two examples of clusters that exist in the camp and that only become apparent when one spends time living inside the camp as an internal observer. The researcher details the nature of these clusters and describes the ways in which they were formed, as well as the different factors that influence them. Certain clusters, for example, are based on the aggregation of related families and their seclusion from other tents; other clusters are formed through the solid relationships that emerge between neighboring tents, which in a way become secluded from their environment.

In studying the third level (the camp and its periphery), the researcher explores refugees' attitudes towards the open spaces generated by the overall urban environment of the camp (surrounding streets, roads between tents, markets and shops), as well as refugees' movements within these spaces, according to their roles and needs and the way they relate to these spaces. The researcher also tries to identify the invisible boundaries that the camp forms between its various components and with its environment.

At the end of this paper, a series of findings regarding the effect of these open spaces on the nature of public and private relationships formed in the camp is presented, by focusing on the role of women and children in particular and how they influence and are influenced by the public space. Men and children are almost entirely in control of public spaces, while women dominate private spaces. Men can be seen roaming the camp throughout the day without any restriction on their mobility, while invisible boundaries affect women much more than men, constraining their movements during the day.

The paper by no means claims that these findings offer an absolute formula to understand the relationships that exist within the camp in general. Rather, it analyses certain case studies at the level of the family or cluster and detects differences in the structure of relationships within the family and with the environment, keeping in mind that these differences are usually the result of variances in the culture and frame of reference of each family. The different social and cultural backgrounds of families and individuals living in the camp are also taken into account, as they reflect the traditions of the various regions of Syria from which the refugee families hail. The paper also attempts to detect the changes that have occurred in these cultures as a result of their contact with each other during this exceptional and compulsory situation, especially with regard to the role of women in public life. In this regard, the researcher has noticed that the role of women is developing in the camp's clusters due to the fact that different families are living in close proximity to one another. By contrast, women play a much less prominent role in clusters that consist of one family for example.

Introduction

Syrian citizens have been relocating to neighbouring countries and elsewhere in an attempt to flee the violence and insecurity of war at home. According to the United Nations High Commissioner for Refugees (UNHCR), the number of Syrian refugees has exceeded three million people scattered around the world, with Lebanon hosting the largest number, recorded at approximately 1.5 million individuals[1] in 2015. However, Lebanon has yet to sign the 1951 Convention that regulates the status of refugees, thus offering little or no protection in comparison to other countries party to the Convention. This has caused different manifestations at all levels, which are most visible in the architectural environment created by refugees themselves. In order to live in camps, Syrian refugees have to pay rent to landowners and build basic housing infrastructure themselves, pitching their tents out of the materials sporadically provided by various organisations. As a result, the shape of these camps is directly dependent on the types of materials supplied by the organisations and the way the refugees use them.

With the exacerbation of the refugee crisis, and after more than four years of displacement of Syrians into neighbouring countries, it has become increasingly necessary to find solutions for the housing of refugees in a way that is responsive to their financial, social and cultural needs. Given the overall context, it is important to analyse and identify the different challenges faced by refugees in order to better understand their critical cultural and social needs, as well as their day-to-day financial needs. This research paper seeks to analyse one component of this environment by looking at how refugees make up the camp's architectural environment, and the visible and invisible cultural and social restraints on the mobility of women and children within it. Women and children were chosen because they constitute the majority of camp residents (women: 26%, children: 52%, men: 22%). The mo-

---

[1]   The statistics are available on the UNHCR website, on the following link https://goo.gl/rAiPRH, noting that the figures mentioned on the website are constantly updated and the abovementioned statistics were reviewed on 25/1/2015.

bility of women is largely tied to and influenced by children, given the nurturing role originally attributed to them in the communities they come from, which continues to impose many constraints on them. This approach was adopted in order to identify the standards that remain priorities for refugees in their architectural environment in conformity with their culture, and to pave the way for a discussion on how this environment can be shaped to create an enabling environment that motivates economic production.

The issues raised in this paper are intended to question how space is formed as an essential social component for refugees, bearing in mind that what is meant by 'space' is the constructed physical and social architectural environment. How do individuals and groups express their identity through this space, particularly in a refugee context?

This paper addresses this issue by assuming that "the space thus produced also serves as a tool of thought and of action," (Lefebvre, 1991) and that "space creates the special relation between function and social meaning in buildings. The ordering of space in buildings is really about the ordering of relations between people." (Hanson, 1984) Consequently, the relationship between human beings, in this case the refugees, and their surroundings not only reflects on their material needs, but also extends to the consideration and fulfilment of their psychological, cultural and social needs. One way of understanding a given society is by examining the spaces it creates and studying their shapes and order. "Through the ways in which buildings, individually and collectively, create and order space, we are able to recognise society: that it exists and has a certain form." (Hillier and Hanson, 1984)

This study is based on research conducted in the Al Jarahiya camp, located in Al Marj, in the western part of Lebanon's Bekaa Valley. This particular camp was selected for the study due to the fact that it is not new, and it continues to grow without being vacated at any stage, contrary to other camps, thus making it relatively stable. This has allowed for greater access in order to trace the characteristics of its architectural environment and their impacts on its residents. In addition to that, Al Jarahiya is a relatively large camp, and its residents come from various regions in Syria. It is worth noting that the study was conducted in the winter of 2015, which has impacted the results. In fact, the need for warmth during the relatively harsh weather conditions had a large influence on daily life. This suggests that components of behaviour or needs in the camp change throughout the year, with the elimination of some factors and the emergence of others, such as not needing to use the stove or being able to keep the windows open for longer periods of time, etc.

The study examines three of the camp's dimensions: the tents, the settlements and the camp as a whole. It also looks into the relationships and mobility of women and children across these three levels, with greater focus on the tent dimension, which is the smallest unit in the camp. Moreover, the research addresses the role of international and local organisations working in the camp in shaping the camp space through the services they provide and the activities they conduct.

For the purposes of this study, the researchers have relied heavily on field visits to the camp and meetings with staff or volunteers in organisations that have a strong presence there. During the visits, the researchers stayed with two families who have been living in the camp for approximately one year and a half. The female members of these two families also facilitated visits to other tents of their female friends and relatives, enabling the researchers to speak to as many residents as possible. Information was collected and recorded during these visits. The researchers were introduced to both families by the *Syrian Eyes* organisation,[2] which has been active in the camp since 2013. This was a major factor in building trust with the families, in addition to our knowledge of their social context and our awareness of the customs and traditions of camp residents during our stay with them.

These two families were chosen as a sample for the study based on several criteria, particularly their willingness to host the researchers and engage in sharing information and perspectives on the camp with them. Also taken into consideration was the selection of two different locations in the camp, with one family living on the periphery of the camp and the other in the centre. Selection criteria also included various characteristics of the family, the number of family members and the nature of their relationships.

---

[2]   For more information about Syrian Eyes organisation, kindly go to: https://goo.gl/rSVWz3.

In order to answer the pivotal question that this paper poses, it was crucial to first determine and study the dynamics and characteristics of the camp. Therefore, the paper studied and identified the key spaces constituting the camp, including those dedicated to general activities and events, and the way they are utilised by residents of the camp. This study also examined the types and forms of housing in the camp, as well as some of the settlement patterns and the reasons why they were formed in this manner. Our aim was to investigate the paths and governing rules of mobility within the spaces in the camp.

We have adopted a descriptive and analytical approach in order to understand how the camp was established and how its physical traits, relationships and social roles have developed. For this reason, the methodology of this paper was based on an ethnographic approach, relying mainly on field visits with primary sources (camp residents), as well as through first-hand experiences and observations in the camp. The written notes that we took during our visits and interviews with the residents were used as primary sources of information. As for qualitative information, we have relied on interactions and discussions with staff or volunteers of Syrian organisations active in the camp, relying on their in-depth knowledge of internal dynamics in the camp.

This paper also references an approach used in a study conducted in the Zaatari camp[3] in Jordan. The researcher studied the camp's architectural environment by collecting reports and surveys on the Zaatari camp, as well as by conducting field visits in order to understand how the camp has developed into a city. Dalal's research includes a comparison between the Zaatari camp and Palestinian camps in the region, with reference to their architectural developments. The study also examines the camp from its establishment and through the different stages of its expansion, as it was conceptually conceived and designed to host large numbers of refugees, in terms of humanitarian access and efficiency, according to a layout elaborated by different organisations.

One of the most interesting points tackled by the Zaatari study was the immensely negative impact felt by refugees from the efforts deployed or work done without consideration of the societal relation-

---

[3]   Ayham Dalal, *Mapping the urbanisation of Zaatari camp*, (Master thesis), Ain Shams University – Egypt and University of Stuttgart – Germany, July 2014.

ships and cultural environment dominant in the camp, thus causing a social shock for residents. One of the implications was modifying the new housing to render it appropriate to their life and culture. The researcher presented several recommendations on how to improve the architecture and its impact on social interactions in a way that is compatible with residents' culture within the camp.

The paper also consulted several sources and studies on architectural environment in order to contextualise the discussion within the framework of theories addressing the formation of an architectural environment and its impact on social life. Moreover, as this paper addresses the concept of the refugee camp as a defined and utilised space, its authors have also relied on Henri Lefebvre's *The Production of Space*, in which the author describes the formation of social spaces in phases. According to Lefebvre, these spaces develop only after being used by those who are most concerned with them, and can only be clearly named as space after their users give them meaning or function.[4] In fact, the final shape and function of a space are not converged upon the end of construction; they are rather acquired after users add symbols to it, whether visible or invisible constraints, and give it a proper name.

During the course of this research, it was difficult to obtain reports written on the Al Jarahiya camp from international organisations. The UNHCR reports that the researcher was able to access only contained information about Al Marj town, without separately providing details on the camp itself. Statistics provided by Save the Children[5] in 2014, combined with information from reports published by INGOs or UN Agencies, offer a general idea about the camp's condition and the history of its formation. The UNHCR has conducted extensive research in this regard, specifically on how best to find adequate solutions for refugee camps to reach standards that provide necessary protection to refugees, as well as creating an enabling environment that facilitates coping and self-reliance. However, the literature and recommenda-

---

[4]   "Space does not exist in itself, it is produced." Goonewardena, Kipfer, Milgrom, Schmid, *Space, Difference, Everyday Life*, Routledge, New York and London, 2008, P. 28

[5]   In order to view the official website of the organisation, kindly click on the following link: https://goo.gl/WbHvis

tions that we were able to access did not take into account the cultural diversity of refugee populations, not to mention that such recommendations could not be implemented in all countries hosting refugees in the same way, but rather remain context-specific.

The study is divided into two sections: the first includes a discussion on the physical description of the camp, highlighting the camp's characteristics, periphery, location and management structure. The second section of this paper details the camp's architectural environment and life within it, starting with the camp's overall structure and settlement patterns, before finally presenting a thorough study of the architectural environment that characterises the tents. This was done by looking at two samples of two tents and at the patterns in which they are settled, and by identifying the relationship between the camp and its periphery at the physical and architectural levels.

The aim of this study is to contribute to finding better methods for organisations to work with refugee communities and to support refugees in ways that are more compatible with their culture. This study also hopes to shed light on issues regarding the impact of the camp's architectural environment on the lives of refugees. We hope that it will be a useful addition to literature on this specific topic, with the belief that work in this field is motivated by the ability to improve refugees' financial and social lives, without clashing in any way with their culture and social norms.

Part One –
Physical Description of the Camp

The Al Jarahiya camp in Lebanon was formed in parallel with the escalation of the conflict in neighbouring Syria, with a marked deterioration of the security and the military context. As Syrians embarked on their forced journey out of their homes and neighbourhoods in search for secure and stable areas, many sought refuge in alternative cities or towns in Syria. Others, however, left the country, fleeing the violence by crossing national borders into Turkey, Jordan or Lebanon. These three neighbouring countries would come to host the largest numbers of Syrian refugees to date. While Egypt and Iraq did accommodate many Syrians and a large number of profiled Syrians were selected for resettlement in several European countries, the number of Syrians outside of neighbouring countries remained relatively low (up to 2015). Most Syrians crossed into and settled in Lebanon, initially forming small settlement communities that soon developed into larger camps throughout the country, most notably in the Bekaa Valley.

The Al Jarahiya camp is located in the Bekaa Valley, near the town of Al Marj, a rural community close to the Lebanese-Syrian border. With the escalation of the conflict in Syria, this area became notably overcrowded with Syrian refugees fleeing violence. Upon arrival in Lebanon, Syrians established random camps scattered throughout the Valley. These settlements were of different sizes, with some consisting of as little as five tents and some up to two hundred tents or more in one camp/settlement area alone. The camp is located near the Al Jarahiya village from which it gets its name. Most of the surrounding lands are used to grow food for livestock, as many residents of the area are sheep and goat herders. It is worth bearing in mind that many Syrian residents of the camp have family or tribal affiliations with Lebanese residents (Bedouins) of Al Jarahiya. Given the village's proximity to the Syrian border, its residents are accustomed to Syrians coming to work in local agricultural production during harvesting season, in addition to the presence of many Syrians amongst the tribes of Al Jarahiya, as they are called by refugees, who herd livestock, crossing constantly between the borders of Lebanon and Syria.

Today, half of the inhabitants of the Al Jarahiya camp come from Homs, while the remaining half are from various locations in Syria, including the Damascus Countryside (Douma, Shebaa, Daraya) and northeast Syria, such as the city of Deir ez-Zor and other high-intensity conflict areas. Al Marj hosts 1247 individuals; 282 men, 312 women and 653 children, living in tents and houses. The majority of the inhabitants of the camp arrived in Lebanon in the first half of 2011. Many Syrians moved around in different areas and camps before finally settling down in the Al Jarahiya camp. The camp initially comprised 67 tents, occupied by 97 families in 2013[6], a number that increased to reach 130 tents inhabited by 180 families as per the statistics of March 2015. A centre and a bakery managed by the organisations *Syrian Eyes* and *Jasmin-Hilfe*[7] were established, in addition to a school jointly managed by the *Sawa*[8] Association and *Jusoor*[9]. At first, several families arrived and pitched tents in the area, expecting their stay to be temporary, and that they would return to their country when the situation inevitably improved. However, reality proved to be quite different, and with the escalation of the armed conflict in Syria in 2013, the number of refugee families spiked. What was at first a few scattered tents has developed into a larger camp housing 180 families, with clear borders and relations between camp residents and their geographic and social periphery. Moreover, a camp management system also emerged internally to regulate relations between the residents and their periphery, as well as the relationship between residents and relief organisations that provide services for the camp. These relations are examined in more detail below.

---

[6] According to *Syrian Eyes* statistics on 27/10/2013

[7] In order to view the official website of the organisation, kindly click on the following link: https://goo.gl/FU1b1P

[8] In order to view the official website of the organisation, kindly click on the following link: https://goo.gl/mHU595

[9] In order to view the official website of the organisation, kindly click on the following link: http://jusoorsyria.com/ar./

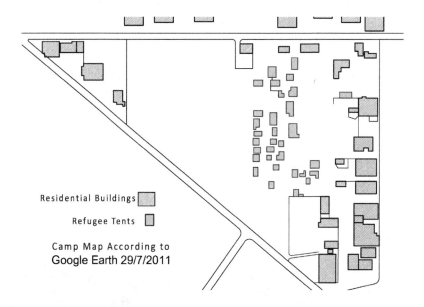

Residential Buildings

Refugee Tents

Camp Map According to
Google Earth 29/7/2011

First – The Periphery

The camp is located in a rural and agricultural area, and as such the town is characterised by its green arable lands mostly used to grow livestock feed. Al Marj is known for its weekly market, open on Mondays near the camp. All basic commodities are sold there, such as fruits, vegetables and other food items, as well as clothing and home supplies. The market extends over a large stretch of land, with steel tented frames blocking off sections into vendor kiosks and stalls erected in the empty spaces between tents.

Many Syrian merchants have previously worked in the market, but their numbers have increased exponentially after the flow of Syrian refugees into Lebanon, so much so that the market has become more Syrian in nature. Several Syrian goods are sold there, and farmers come from nearby Syrian towns close to the border carrying their share of crops to be sold at lower prices than other shops in the area.

The camp is surrounded by many low-rise buildings, characterised by their simplicity and the gardens surrounding them. Some tents receive utility services from the residents of these buildings, who each share their electrical power with a group of tents. In addition to that, women from the camp collect water from the garden faucet of a near-by house whenever their tents run out of clean water.

There is a mosque opposite the camp where men go to pray on Fridays. Nearby, the Al Jarahiya School provides night shift schooling for children of the camp and other neighbouring camps. Despite the fact that the school is close-by, the majority of children take the school bus that picks them up at the entry point of the camp and drops them off at the school gate. Parents prefer their children taking the bus for several reasons: first, they fear for their children's safety in an area that remains unfamiliar to them, despite having lived there for some time now; second, they worry that their children might leave school and come back home, or skip out on school to go play in the camp or in neighbouring areas.

Satellite image of the Al Jarahiya Camp from Google Earth - 2015

Second – Location

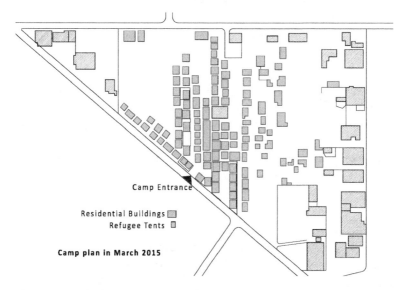

Camp Entrance

Residential Buildings ▢
Refugee Tents ▢

Camp plan in March 2015

The camp is built on two plots of land owned by two relatives, separated by a road that divides the camp in half.

Tents are erected on both sides of the road in two parallel rows. Vertically, the camp is bordered by two roads for cars, and horizontally, it is adjacent to neighbouring residential buildings. Contiguous tents and buildings share certain utility services, such as electrical power and water.

The camp's population is denser and more crowded on the right side, closer to the adjacent residential buildings. This portion of the camp belongs to the landowner who first leased it to incoming refugees. As one moves to the left side of the camp, the number of tents visibly decreases, until one reaches a large empty stretch of land, where only two isolated tents are situated far away from the crowdedness of the rest of the camp.

Most residents of the camp pay rent on an annual basis in exchange for the land on which they erect their tents and live. They pay somewhere between 700,000 and 900,000 Lebanese pounds, equivalent to 466 and 600 USD, with the rent fees varying according to the tent size. Some organisations provide financial assistance to help pay rent fees if families cannot afford them. Around six families live in the camp for free, based on an agreement with the landlords facilitated by mutual acquaintances of Lebanese relatives.

In addition to the tents, there is one house, made of concrete blocks, built at the centre of the camp, belonging to a Syrian family that had purchased the land after coming to Lebanon. Families that do not pay rent have pitched tents around this house.

The tents are organised in parallel vertical lines, thus creating main roads and side roads within the camp, separating each row of tents. In some cases, these side roads are blocked by completely contiguous tents or by tarps or fabric curtains. The tents are so close to one another that they appear to be one big tent, due to the fact that some walls overlap or because the ceiling of one tent's balcony[10] happens to overlay the wall of another. Despite the parallel and quasi-organised alignment of the tents, their locations are not strategically positioned according to pathways and/or roads. When walking along the secondary internal roads, visitors find themselves in a sort of maze, where tent entrances are sometimes hidden, and visitors have to walk around several tents to eventually find the entrance to the one they were previously standing next to.

Every tent has one water tank nearby, and a very small number have two, provided by World Vision[11] and the United Nations. World Vision is responsible for filling these tanks with clean water once or twice per week. Each tent is also equipped with a metal latrine, including a squat toilet, provided by UNICEF. The latrine is located either in the outer space of the tent or inside, within the spot allocated for the bathroom, and is connected to a pit for waste collection. World Vision is committed to cleaning the pits weekly, but there are often delays.

Several plots of land remain empty and are scattered around three peripheral areas of the camp. They are mainly used for livestock herding: some refugees continue to work as herders as they did in Syria. Several families raise poultry as well, and oftentimes those living close to the empty lands allow their chickens to roam freely during the day.

---

[10] Balcony: Empty space that is part of the tent, connected to its entrance and separating the rooms from the exterior streets. It is often without a ceiling and open on one of its sides which is connected to the exterior. We will explain the functions of the balcony in the section on tents.

[11] In order to view the official website of the organisation, kindly click on the following link: https://www.worldvision.org

These stretches of land have no other use since they are covered with livestock faeces and chicken feed. They also have holes in the ground caused by livestock hooves. Previously, the middle yard had been used as a playground for children, where they spent hours and hours playing football and other games. However, this space has consistently shrunk due to the increasing number of tents being crammed around it, rendering it smaller and dirtier, and making it impossible to use as a playground.

At the entry point to the camp, there is a children school that was established by the *Jusoor* and *Sawa* organisations. The school takes up two tents and is surrounded by a fence. It provides one morning shift, which accommodates both boys and girls up until ninth grade.

The school was founded in March 2014 in order to provide for children who were unable to enrol in Lebanese schools due to government-imposed restrictions, as well as for children whose parents were uneasy with the idea of sending them off to schools far from the camp. At the structural level, the school tent does not differ much from the surrounding residential tents, and is only characterised by the surrounding fence that is locked with padlock, as well as by the drawings decorating the walls, indicating that it is a school or a space dedicated for children.

In addition to the above, the *Syrian Eyes* and *Jasmin-Helfi* organisations have established a community centre that holds activities in the camp. The tent designated for the centre is divided into two sections, with two separate doors on the main road of the camp. The first section has two rooms: the first is mostly used as a warehouse for relief items, whereas the second is a children's activity centre that offers a morning shift for preschool children and children aged 7 or below.

A female camp resident with a background in teaching works at the centre, which promotes the role of women living in the camp and empowers them to be self-reliant. The centre closes at night and can be used for different logistical or administrative work carried out by the staff of *Syrian Eyes* whenever they visit the camp.

In the second section of the tent, there is a medical clinic managed by a Syrian physician, who is himself a refugee, although living outside the camp. The clinic operates for three hours, three days per week, and provides medical consultations for camp residents, in addition to free medication when available.

Syrian Eyes and *Jasmin-Helfi* have also established a Saj (flatbread) bakery at the camp. The flatbread oven was officially launched in February. So far, the bakery has been opening daily, and women from the camp knead and bake the dough, and bread is later distributed to camp residents at a reduced price. The bakery is equipped only with basic machinery, without much sophistication in its structure or space. In fact, it only features one electrical kneading machine, two large gas-operated flatbread ovens and a long board to knead and prepare bread loaves.

Al Jarahiya camp is one of the largest Syrian camps in Lebanon, based on the number of residents. This has required the elaboration of a simple management system in order to facilitate communication among residents themselves and between residents and relief organisations and institutions providing services and assistance, as well as between the camp's residents and its periphery.

Third – Camp Management

International organisations are normally responsible for overseeing refugee camps and managing needs and services. However, since the Lebanese state has not signed the 1951 Convention and Protocol Relating to the Status of Refugees, mandated organisations face significant legal and operational restrictions in managing the camps. Their intervention in the Al Jarahiya camp includes providing residents with raw materials for construction, distributing limited relief items and taking care of sanitation and drafting water.

International organisations operating in the Al Jarahiya camp inculde: UNHCR, World Vision, War Child, Save the Children and Jasmin-Helfi. Lebanese and Syrian organisations are also active in the camp and include: Syrian Eyes and the Sawa and Jusoor associations. World Vision is in charge of sanitation, waste disposal and the provision of drinking water, while Save the Children and Syrian Eyes provide tent equipment, such as wood and covers, and lay gravel between tents. UNHCR provides camp residents with metal latrines and water tanks.

Jusoor and Sawa have established and currently manage a school situated in the camp. Syrian Eyes has established a medical clinic, a children's activity centre and a bakery.

Generally-speaking, organisations working at Syrian refugee camps manage the relationship with camp residents through a 'representative' from the camp, considered as a focal point or go-between. This person is referred to as the "*Shawish*". Although there are several disadvantages to this mode of operation, mediators or "*Shawish*" largely facilitate the work of organisations inside the camps.

Among the several disadvantages of this system is the likelihood of corruption and the ability of the *Shawish* to use this position of authority for personal interests, or even to favour relatives and acquaintances over fair distribution among camp residents. Nevertheless, the *Shawish* system greatly contributes to a better understanding of the needs of camp residents, voiced directly by concerned individuals. *Shawishs* are also able to assist in mutual dialogue, as they are keen to attend events and occasions taking place in the camp and better poised to communicate back with camp residents in a way that is familiar to them. Finally, *Shawishs* can offer inside knowledge of hidden facts or issues that camp residents may try to cover up. By doing so, they largely act as informants for external actors on camp goings-on.

The *Shawish* is often chosen by camp residents to play the role of intermediary between the camp and external actors. This selection process differs between camps: in some cases, a person may be named "*Shawish*" due to their financial prowess and/or their direct relationship with the landlord; in other cases, the *Shawish* may be appointed based on their family lineage or because they are the leader of a large and important or powerful family in the camp.

At Al Jarahiya camp, there are two *Shawishs* who were selected due to their close relationship with several families in the camp, as well as their strong relationship with organisations that are active at the camp. These two individuals regulate the organisations' relationship with camp residents and assist in aid distribution based on the needs of each and every family. They also help in collecting documentation from camp residents and holding various activities at the camp.

The main advantage of the *Shawish* system in this particular camp is that the authority of the *Shawish* remains limited to service provision in collaboration with organisations, with occasional interventions to settle disputes between camp residents. Both "*Shawishs*" at Al Jarahiya were greatly collaborative during this research, in terms of providing information and facilitating communication with camp residents. Naturally, some individuals in the camp expressed dissatisfaction with the role of the *Shawish* or stated that the *Shawishs* do not provide enough support for the camp. However, based on observation, and according to testimonies from most of the residents, it was clear that both *Shawishs* at Al Jarahiya went to great lengths to be as supportive and helpful as possible.

In addition to the *Shawish* system, camp residents also play a role in organising their own communications and interactions. Every group of tents selects one individual to communicate with the two *Shawishs* and provide them with necessary information on activities within the camp. The tasks of this individual consist of transmitting information and making requests related to the needs of the tents they represent. The *Shawish* can refuse a request if they discover that it is unfounded or is an attempt to take advantage of the situation rather than meet a specific need. Cases where a *Shawish* might reject a request include, for instance, a family asking for an additional share of firewood despite having a sufficient quantity, while other families have not yet obtained their shares. Ties between these groups of tents are often built on kinship of the first and second degrees. The eldest male of the family is in charge of its affairs, as family relationships at the camp are governed by patriarchal regime[12]. This male dominance may be broken, and a woman may take charge of family affairs if the man is absent, given the ongoing need to communicate and provide for the family. One example of such a situation is a camp family from rural Damascus, where a woman in her sixties came to Lebanon with two of her sons, her two daughters and their children, but without her husband, making her effectively in charge of her family's affairs. This clearly indicates that camp management responsibilities are shared among residents. It also illustrates that the camp is divided into clusters of tents that enjoy closer ties with each other than with remaining residents, and this is

---

[12]   "Patriarchy in its wider definition means the manifestation and institutionalization of male dominance over women and children in the family and the extension of male dominance over women in society in general." (Lerner, 1986)

evident through the fact that the individuals in charge are nominated by the clusters of tents, rather than by a third party from inside or outside the camp.

The communication system established between residents and organisations operating in the camp is a local administration model specific to the camp. Interestingly, this model is itself derived from the material and social needs and requirements of refugees and is influenced by their capacities. In other words, the refugees themselves have developed a model of life inside the camp and they did so based on the resources available to them and according to the basic needs and habits of their community, without any considerable outside intervention imposing a specific way to shape this space. This includes how the inside of the tents is designed, how the tents themselves are distributed and how pathways and roads are constructed or delineated between and around tent clusters. While the research paper studies these different camp spaces, it also takes into consideration that it is not enough to merely identify the names or functions of the spaces. We must understand how this space is utilised by residents themselves, how they spend their time in it and what restraints and implications they insert to this space through their actions, thus giving it its ultimate meaning. All of this requires defining the nature of the camp's architectural environment, starting from the periphery and the borders of the camp, to the settlement clusters and tents with all their characteristics and peculiarities, as well as their impact on the lives of refugees.

Part Two –
Architectural Environment of the Camp and Life in It

This section will examine the architectural environment of the Al Jarahiya camp and the life of its refugees. It will first examine the general architectural environment of the camp, before moving on to its settlements, clusters and tents. We will also present samples of families and use these case studies to illustrate how they interact and deal with both public and private spaces within the camp.

During field visits, our research methodology relied on documenting and drawing the camp layout on several scales. The larger scale incorporates the entire camp and its periphery, followed by the medium scale, where we focus on two samples of clusters with different social and physical visible traits. Finally, the smallest scale consists of samples of tents located in the mentioned clusters.

Through our examination of both tents, we were able to observe the following family dynamics: first, a family consisting of adult single siblings, in which the men are employed outside the home and the women work inside the home. The second sample consists of two families, where the women are sisters, and each family lives in one room. The first sister's family is comprised of a mother, a father and six children between the ages of one and sixteen years. The father is currently employed and the mother has recently started working at the camp's bakery. The other family includes the second sister, who is a single mother, and her two daughters (fifteen and sixteen years old). Therefore, the study was based on the observation of these three cases within in the camp structure.

During field visits, and at different stages of the study, researchers counted the tents in every row and identified their most important physical components. Then, during the time available for work at the camp, these observations were incorporated into the layout, with the narratives and commentary gathered from the refugees themselves. This was all finalised and complemented with the researchers' personal observations, drawn from their presence in the camp and their take on life inside of it.

In his book, *The Poetics of Space*, Gaston Bachelard characterises the importance of the 'home' as (wo)man's basic shelter and the space in which he/she feels safe. One can examine this in the context of refugee camps, given their innate vulnerability and inability to provide safety and protection at the material level.[13] Bachelard also discusses how a man/woman builds thick protective walls when such a home is non-existent, an act that reflects, at its core, a desire to protect the house that is, or represents, a home.[14] In fact, due to the near absence of real safety and protection mechanisms in camps, camp residents resort to building protective walls, which must be taken into consideration and left unharmed during any intervention in the camp structure, with inevitable reverberations on the camp's architectural and social fabric.

Therefore, it is crucial not to ignore any component or characteristic that residents add to the architectural environment of the camp. It is also of equal importance to understand each and every detail of the camp, no matter how small it might seem, due to the fact that its inclusion in the camp was an intentional act by refugees. Similarly, studying where refugees place these details could provide significant insight. Furthermore, it is essential to examine both the spaces that can be visibly perceived (or are quite obvious by nature) and those that are reflected more subtly through actions that erect invisible boundaries, as these latter are of equal importance.

---

[13]   "The house shelters day dreaming, the house protects the dreamer, the house allows dreaming, the house protects the dreamer." Bachelard G, *The Poetics of Space*, translated from the French by Maria Jolas, Beacon Press Boston, 1994, P.6

[14]   "All really inhabited space bears the essence of the notion of home. In course of this work, we shall see that the imagination builds? "walls" of impalpable shadows, comforts? Itself with the illusion of protection or, just the contrary, trembles? behind thick walls" The previous reference, P.5

Alina Oueishek – Al Jarahiya Camp – Lebanon – 2015

First – The Camp's General Structure

From the outside, the camp appears to be a large mass of different coloured tarps, decorated with electric wires and water tanks placed on wooden poles. At first glance, it seems to be composed of a few long, extended tents, and the traces of a few windows closed by sheets or covers can seldom be seen along these long facades.

Many of these tents are surrounded by low fences of wood and metal wires, which form an outdoor terrace space, also called "balconies" by the residents. Therefore, this paper will also use the term "balcony" when referring to this outdoor space.

Save the Children and *Syrian Eyes* have implemented a project to pave the internal roads with gravel, while several secondary roads and empty spaces remain uncovered. As such, unpaved roads often become muddy and impossible to walk on during winter. For this reason, refugees resort, insofar as they are able, to lining some roads with gravel bags as a low and makeshift sidewalk.

The tents are erected on a concrete platform laid directly on the floor without any anchors or foundation. This provides hard flooring for the tent, protecting it from rain during winter and from other external factors. However, residents have made the unfortunate mistake of using low platforms, not being aware of the nature of the land and weather in the area, and this has put their tents at risk of flooding in the winter.

Lebanon has not signed the Convention and Protocol Relating to the Status of Refugees and still fears the recurrence of the experience of Palestinian camps. This has had a great impact on the structure of Syrian refugee camps. For one, the Lebanese government has not formally established any camps, nor allocated lands for them. The Lebanese state's intervention was rather limited to issuing rules, still outside the scope of formal law, to organise the construction of tents. It did so in coordination with the United Nations and other mandated organisations. According to these rules issued by the Lebanese government and agreed upon with the UN, digging holes and laying deep foundations was to be absolutely prohibited, and so was using concrete blocks that exceed 40 cm in height. Wood and zinc were identified as the materials to be used for the covers, while metal was also prohibited.

According to previous agreements, all camps in Lebanon must be slightly uniform in their construction, with rare instances of residents actually violating the regulations and building their tents out of concrete. However, no such cases were observed at the Al Jarahiya camp. The majority of the tents in Al Jarahiya are built out of wood with an added cover, with some of the tents using zinc planks for walls. The wooden frames are made up of poles, and support materials are erected directly on the concrete platform or on top of blocks simply placed on top of it. They are then covered with plain plastic sheeting, sometimes including thin wooden planks, to form internal and external walls.

The covers used vary in terms of size, colour and material. Oftentimes, these covers are made out of advertisement boards of sorts or sheeting that carry the names or logos of international organisations such as UNHCR and World Vision, among others. Car wheels are put over the gabled ceilings to prevent them from being blown away.

As for the windows, residents usually leave spaces between wooden planks or cut out openings in the sheeting and then cover them to keep the windows closed. In rare instances, mobile wooden planks are used to open or close the window as needed, or transparent plastic items are used to cover openings. Based on our observations, it was clear that all tents have external doors that are mostly without door handles, and can be additionally locked for protection, whereas internal doors remain a luxury, and are substituted by sheets in order to cover the openings separating internal spaces. As for internal walls, they are often made out of covers, without wooden support, in order to save the planks of wood, whenever available, to cover external walls for added protection against harsh weather. Metal latrines are located either inside the tents in the bathroom area, or outside in the open air, within the confines of the balcony of each tent. When outside, the latrines are placed in a way that put the door at the furthest point from public space in front of the tent, forcing tent residents to go around the tent in order to reach the door, hidden from passers-by.

The current physical shape of the tents does not provide any form of safety or protection. The materials permitted for building, i.e. untreated wood, plastic and fabric, are flammable and lightweight materials. They are not water-repellent and can easily sustain physical damage. The tents fabricated from these materials can be easily broken into by an intruder, since they are extremely vulnerable and their walls are more token than functional in terms of insulation and protection. In addition to the fact that they provide no protection against the elements and intrusion, the thin walls of the tents are not soundproof, and therefore cannot protect the privacy of the families. Not only do they offer no physical protection, but they also interfere with social relations and the degree of privacy of any family from the surrounding community.

Since tarps are the most widely available material, they are used for most interior and exterior walls and have become the main material for wall-building. Thin MDF wood panels are sometimes added to these walls, but they rarely cover entire walls and they remain hidden, without appearing on the external façades of the tent. As a result, the façades of these tents appear as a single mass of coloured tarps patched together and extending across the entire camp. This façade is devoid of its resident's identity; it is prevalently characterised by the two identities of randomness, visible in the content and shapes of advertisement boards and of the refugee status, reflected through the logos of the aid organisations.

Alina Oueishek – Al Jarahiya Camp – Lebanon – 2015

Second – The Tent

"An entire past comes to dwell in a new house."[15]

This section examines the smallest unit in the camp: the tent itself. Researchers have shared this space with camp residents during field visits and, through that experience, were able to closely identify its components, as well as its physical and social determinants. Most of the tents are composed of one living room, used for all daily activities. Very few tents have two rooms, and not a single tent with three rooms was found during visits to the camp.

The section below provides a review of the most important elements observed, presented in a detailed study of two tents in which researchers were able to stay during field visits. These two examples showcase the components of the tent and the items found within it, in addition to the lifestyle of every family member within the tent space, including their use of the space and the delimitation and distribution of roles within this space. Two different cases were studied with re-

---

[15]   Bachelard G, *The Poetics of Space*, translated from the French by Maria Jolas, Beacon Press, Boston, 1994, P. 5

gards to family composition: the first tent is occupied by siblings with no children, and the second tent by two sisters and their children.

1 – Tent (A)

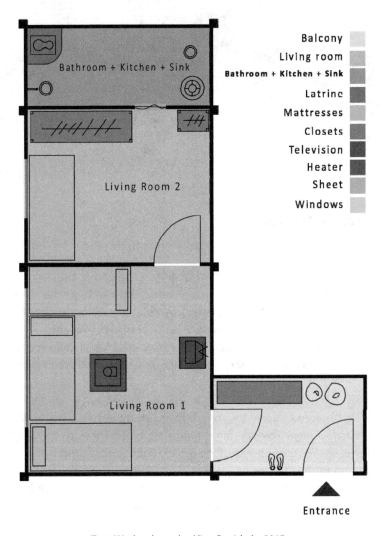

Tent (A) plan drawn by Alina Oueishek - 2015

A family of three brothers and one sister lives in tent (A). They all come from the Al Bayada village in Homs, where they used to live with their parents in a multi-storey building. After the deterioration of the situation in Al Bayada in 2011, the family came to Lebanon, first settling in Tripoli. After several relocations from one camp to another, and from one house to another, the family finally settled down in the Al Jarahiya camp. They built their current tent in December 2015, approximately one month prior to the beginning of this field study.

The family includes a second sister who left her siblings and returned to Syria, leaving only one sister in the camp with her three brothers.

Tent (A) comprises four main spaces: the balcony, two living rooms and a bathroom with a kitchen and a latrine. These spaces are separated by covers and piece of wood fixed on wooden poles, or simply with pieces of cloth functioning as doors. The flooring is paved with concrete and is elevated from the outside ground level, forming a hard platform for the rooms and preventing water from leaking inside during winter.

The balcony is the initial space before entering the tent itself. It is used to place shoes and store firewood for winter. Despite having two rooms, the researchers only observed one room being used for all activities during field visits. This room has a wood stove and television, while the second living space is used for cooking. The bathroom is located with the kitchen at the end of the tent and is separated from the living room by a sheet of fabric. The bathroom space is used for showering, cooking and washing the dishes, and all necessary equipment is available in this space. It is normally wet, as opposed to other parts of the house, which are usually drier.

The tent has the basic necessities of life; there is no exaggeration or clutter of unnecessary items. Every room contains the essential items used in daily life: both living rooms are covered with mats and carpets, distinguishing them from other spaces in the house as clean and dry spaces. The first living room has three mattresses, laid down in the shape of an open rectangle, with the wood stove in the middle, facing a small table for the television and receiver. There is only one power socket in the room, and an extension cord with several plugs is used for all electrical supplies in the home.

There are no decorative or aesthetic items in the room, and the wooden sheets of random colours and shapes placed around the tent as walls are clearly visible.

The second room is similar to the first one in its size and composition: the floor is covered with mats, and wooden walls are fixed on poles. This room has two closets facing the entrance; one small cabinet for food supplies and another larger cabinet for covers, sheets and clothing. Unlike the television table in the living room that the family bought ready-made, these cabinets were homemade using available materials, such as simple wooden poles, with fixed shelves without doors or paint. The family covers these closets with a sheet to put away or hide their contents.

This room is directly linked to the bathroom and cooking space, only separated by a sheet used as a makeshift door.

The concrete bathroom floor is not covered and remains wet most of the day. It is sloped downwards towards the squat toilet where water is drained. The bathroom space includes a small gas heater, with a metal vessel next to it used to collect and wash dirty dishes. On the other side, there is a water faucet with the washing bucket.

The metal latrine is located in the farthest corner of the room, with the squat toilet placed above a waste collection pit.

The main room is used for daily activities. It transforms from a living room into a dining room, a salon for guests and a bedroom when the day comes to an end. The mattresses in it are used for various purposes: when the activity changes, residents simply add or remove items. In fact, the day starts by tidying the sheets and quilts and putting them in the closet in the other room, thus turning the space back into a living room, after being used as a bedroom during night-time. Whenever it is time for a main meal, a nylon sheet is placed on the ground, transforming the room into a dining space with a table where the food tray is laid down.

The stove remains at the centre of all these activities, since family members sit around it while socialising together.

The sister spends most of her time in the tent, busying herself with 'keeping house', cleaning and tidying up, whereas the brothers spend the majority of their day at work. During the day, the tent turns into an almost exclusively female space: the woman's relatives come over to visit, socialise and talk about their daily lives, children, etc., all the while taking a break from household chores. Consequently, during daytime, the tent becomes the kingdom of the women of the camp, where they are in charge and do all the work, and where the brothers' role is consumptive. Although the brothers also socialise with families in the camp and spend significant amounts of time in their tents, the sister spends most of her day there. She is not really allowed to go anywhere, other than what she calls "inside the camp", and so remains the most attached to the tent.

2 – Tent (B)

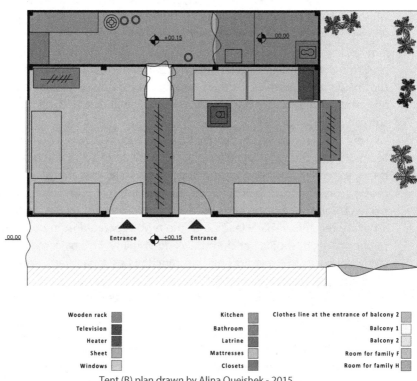

Wooden rack		Kitchen		Clothes line at the entrance of balcony 2	
Television		Bathroom		Balcony 1	
Heater		Latrine		Balcony 2	
Sheet		Mattresses		Room for family F	
Windows		Closets		Room for family H	

Tent (B) plan drawn by Alina Oueishek - 2015

Two siblings and their nuclear families live in tent (B): one sister (H) with her husband and six children, three boys and three girls, between the ages of seven months and fourteen, and the other (F), who is a long-time divorcee, with her two daughters, aged eighteen and six-teen years old.

Encouraged by their father to leave Syria, they both came to Leba-non in 2011 and initially stayed in a house near the camp. However, basic sanitary conditions were very poor at the house, which led the sisters to move to the camp. Upon their arrival, they built their tent on a piece of land they were able to secure rent-free, through social ac-quaintances linked to the landlord.

Both families came from Shebaa, in Damascus Countryside, where they had lived their entire lives before seeking refuge in Lebanon. (H) lived in a multi-storey house with her husband in Shebaa, with sur-rounding farms owned by her family. As for (F), she had been living with her daughters in her parents' traditional house since she got di-vorced. Divorced women are subject to greater constraints in Syrian families in general, especially in the area from which the camp families hail. This is ascribed to the customs and traditions that impose the re-turn of divorced women to their parents' household and their con-finement to the house, due to considerable prejudice and negative stereotypes against them.

Tent (B) is composed of six main spaces: two balconies, two living rooms, one kitchen and one bathroom with the latrine. The tent has no doors, except for the wooden entrance doors that separate the living rooms from the front balcony, whereas the internal rooms are con-nected through sheets of fabric used as doors. One balcony is a kind of a private reception space leading to the tent, separated from outside public spaces by a piece of cloth blocking visibility. This balcony is di-rectly linked to the second one that functions as a backyard, where residents grow plants during summer.

Each family lives in a separate room with an independent door that leads to the balcony. A closet is used as a wall to separate the rooms, with a square corridor next to it, leading to the shared kitchen and bathroom. All three rooms around this corridor are sectioned off by hanging sheets of cloth.

The floor of family (B)'s room is covered with cardboard, with large carpets on top, over an uneven concrete ground. During the day, there are three mattresses that form an open square, at one end of which the wood stove is located. The television is situated on top of a wooden rack in one of the corners and is plugged into the only power socket in the room. A swing dangles from one of the wooden frames closest to the wall and can be pulled out and fixed up against the wall when not in use, leaving an empty space in the room. Moreover, family (B) uses the separating closet to store mattresses that are not used during the day, in addition to other items such as clothes and a few personal belongings. This closet is made of simple wooden poles with racks fixed to them, covered with a fabric sheet to put away its contents.

The floor of the second room, room (F), is carpeted without a cardboard layer, because the ground is more even and does not require additional levelling. Over the carpets are two perpendicular mattresses, in addition to a makeshift closet made up of piled blankets on a small table and covered with a sheet to be put away with the contents.

Opposite the entrance door is the only power socket in the room, located slightly above a wooden rack, where a mirror is sometimes placed. This room has no stove or television; rather, only the items necessary for either sitting, lounging or sleeping can be found here. Walls in both rooms are decorated with curtains. While the curtains do offer an aesthetic touch, they also provide additional protection from the cold, since they make up an extra layer of insulation over the external walls.

During winter, one can seldom see the windows, as all residents cover them to protect their tents against the cold, making the internal space more sombre, with little light coming in, day or night.

The common kitchen space includes a large wooden shelf used for cooking and storing items, as well as a cabinet high up on the wall perpendicular to it, also used to store food supplies, dishes and glasses. Next to the shelf and opposite the entrance from the corridor (closed with a fabric curtain), one sees the gas stove, as well as two buckets filled with water used for cleaning or washing, since the tent is not equipped with a faucet. The buckets are filled using a hose coming from the water tank into the kitchen, through the window. Within the same space and opposite the kitchen, one finds the bathroom and latrine, separated from the kitchen by a large curtain. This curtain remains open most of the day, except for when a member of the two households needs to use the bathroom or the latrine.

Both women spend the day together in one room, usually (H)'s room, as it includes a heater. As for the children of the two families, they are either in the tent or at school. The youngest, a seven-month-old boy, stays with his mother, his aunt or his female cousins who take care of him all day and rarely leave him unattended. Overall, if the children of household (H) do not have school, or have spare time after school, the girls and the seven-year-old boy spend the day inside the tent with their mother. However, the oldest child, a fourteen-year-old boy, spends most of his time outside the tent with his friends, and does not come home before dusk, when the camp gets dark.

Women most often keep their hijab on when inside; sometimes younger girls can loosen it a bit, but they rarely take it off altogether, just in case a male visitor passes by or visits suddenly, in which case they would have to put it back it on again quickly.

When the women host other female visitors, regardless of whether they are from inside or outside of the camp, the husband of household (H) would be obliged to leave the tent and go visit a neighbour or friend, in order to give the women their privacy. The women then feel comfortable to remove the hijab. Children also feel happy when the tent becomes an exclusively female space, as men can no longer enter without permission.

Having both families in one tent strengthens the familial bond between them. In fact, the daughters of (F) often take care of their younger cousins and help care for the seven-month-old baby, and it is them who put him to bed. Needless to say, with the absence of any walls or soundproof doors, the girls cannot avoid putting the baby to bed when their aunt asks them to do so. However, the girls have become so attached to their baby cousin that they refer to him as their own baby and want to raise him themselves. This is, in fact, the reality of the situation, even if the matter can be discussed lightly.

3 – The Tent

Women dominate the internal spaces of the tent. Since the function of women in their societies of origin is frequently tied to their reproductive role, they spend most of their time inside and are in charge of housekeeping and raising children. The husband's role in the tent is restricted to repair works; outside the tent, however, they assume social and economic responsibilities. Women's participation outside the house varies based on the areas from which they come and on their specific customs, as well as on their age and social status. Women from Aleppo and Homs are more tied to the house than those coming from Shebaa and Bayada, who work alongside men in agriculture and tending the livestock[16]. However, it is worth noting that these activities are not considered as 'work' by society and by the family, since they are undertaken as part of the family business and property. There are also more restrictions on divorced women than on unmarried women. In spite of these dynamics, the extraordinary circumstances experienced by families living in refugee camps have imposed changes in these gender roles, particularly when no men are present in the family or when the men are unable to provide for the family by themselves. Women are often forced to visit UN facilities to collect their family's relief. In some rare cases discussed later on in the study, women have sought employment. Although these functions are added to women's responsibilities towards their households and children, they have contributed to breaking the gender role imposed by society and have helped to create new experiences and to extend women's participation in the camp's public spaces.

According to the interviewed women, and based on the observations of the researchers during the visits, children under the age of seven remain attached to their mothers wherever they may be, and boys gain more freedom in their mobility after the age of eight, whereas around this age, girls start helping their mothers with household chores. Based on the interviews with the women, girls stay inside the tent for several reasons, including the fact that interaction between girls and boys outside the family is frowned upon, especially as girls approach puberty. This stems from regional customs and traditions, as well as the wish to protect girls from unknown boys and men and to preserve their reputation and honour. Girls thus begin to learn and practice their housekeeping role. The age at which the mobility of girls begins to be restricted varies depending on each area's specific customs. Some girls insist on playing with other children outside and

---

[16]   This information was gathered from the statements of interviewed women about their previous lives in their hometowns in Syria, in addition to a collection of photographs that they showed to the researcher.

may be allowed to go out once or twice per week. However, the time they spend playing steadily decreases as they grow older, until the age of thirteen, when girls in most families are no longer allowed to play outside. Girls are pressured by their parents and their immediate community through moral, societal and religious justifications to refrain from playing outside or interacting with boys, and they are encouraged to begin helping their mothers. In some families, girls are married off when they turn thirteen. During one of our visits to the camp, we witnessed the wedding of a girl who was married off due to the social customs prevalent in her family's hometown, where girls do not finish their studies and are married off early on. Another factor contributing to early marriage is the family's poor financial situation, as the financial responsibility for the girl is transferred to her husband after marriage. Families from certain regions allow girls to pursue their education, but the inability to enrol children in Grade 10 in Lebanon limits this capacity. As a result, girls are unable to benefit from this opportunity, and they spend longer periods at home. For this reason, the availability of vocational training courses and projects for women and girls at the camp helps them to participate in public life.

During field visits, the researchers became aware of the importance of the heater in identifying the living space. In fact, despite the presence of more than one room in the tent, the only room used throughout the day is the heated one, while the others are used more rarely and for very specific functions. The heater also plays a pivotal role in ensuring the independence of one family from another one living in the same tent.

In one of the field visits, one family got a new heater. This was cause for celebration, as it gave the family true independence from the in-laws. Although both families continued to cook and eat together, the presence of an additional heater gave family members the option of spending their day separately if they so choose, without being physically confined to one space.

The balcony is considered a very important element of the tent as well, especially for female residents. The researchers noticed that most families have a balcony, even if it is just a small one. During visits to the camp, one family added covers to the ceiling of the front balcony leading to their tent, stating that it belonged to their tent and was their private space. Moreover, refugees tried to recreate miniature farms similar to their homes in Syria. As most camp residents come from rural areas, they are used to owning and working in farms around their homes, spending most of their time there or in public ones nearby. Since these farms are part of the house, women can move about them unconstrained, unless there are guests from outside the family. For this reason, these makeshift farms give women a private space outside the walls of the house. Balconies allow for this added mobility at the camp and provide an outdoor space, in addition to the indoor space of the tent. During summer, women plant different kinds of greeneries and flowers in the balconies, turning them into cosy living spaces, where families spend most of their daytime. Bachelard offers insight on the relationship of the house-dweller to the objects therein, stating that "Objects that are cherished in this way really are born of an intimate light, and they attain to a higher degree of reality than indifferent objects, or those that are defined by geometric reality."[17] In this light, the amount of care given by women to these balconies transforms them into real balconies and farms, reminiscent of the ones they left behind in their abandoned homes.

Third – The Clusters

> "Social space is what permits fresh actions to occur, while suggesting others and prohibiting yet others."[18]

This section illustrates various types of clusters one might find in the camp, by examining two cases: the first case being in the middle of the camp, including tent (B), and the second one located at the far end of the camp, including tent (A). Although these clusters are not visible to the outside observer, after spending some time in the camp, an inside observer would clearly begin to identify them. The clusters are the result of several factors, such as the congregation and seclusion of related families, as well as the tight relationships that bring families residing in neighbouring tents together. At times, this cluster layout isolates families, in one way or another, from the remainder of the camp.

---

[17]   Bachelard, 1994
[18]   *The Production of Space*, Foregoing reference, P. 73

1 – Cluster A

Cluster (A) includes tent (B) and a number of other tents. It has no visible or physical barrier, but is rather based on the type of relationship that exists between the families that live within its confines. These families live either in tents at the farthermost end of the camp or in tents outside the camp altogether, or even in apartments opposite the camp. Tent (B) is located at the far end of the camp and therefore has less contact with the tents and families of the other cluster. Due to its location, it is easier for the residents of Tent (B) to choose the families they come into contact with, mostly because neighbouring tents are erected several meters away, and (B) is surrounded by large unused spaces, whereas the other tents in the camp are contiguous.

Facing tent (B) directly is tent (A), inhabited by a female relative of the first family, who came to the camp approximately one month prior to the first field visit. Tent (A) family members chose to relocate to this camp for many reasons, but their move was predominantly due to the insecurity they felt in their former place of residence. They chose a piece of land that is adjacent to that of their relatives and erected their new tent there. The newcomers repeatedly mentioned that the area they used to live in was perhaps more visually appealing and was better suited to fulfil their daily needs. However, they clearly expressed their desire to move to a more secure area. Tent (A) followed the lead of other family members, and now some of their more distant relatives have come to live in the same area.

Two other families live outside the camp on the opposite street.

In tents (A) and (B), families are next-door neighbours: one family lives in an apartment in an unfinished building opposite the camp, and the second in a tent adjacent to the building.

The women of both families spend most of their day together, as they are not allowed to socialise with other women in the camp. Their relationships are confined to family members. Despite having friendships with Arab Bedouin Lebanese women who live in the building adjacent to the camp, the scope of this relationship is defined by the male members of the family, including the larger family unit.

Despite the fact that the male members of the aforementioned families actively interact or have relationships with other families at the camp, and despite the fact that they frequently pay visits to various homes/tents, there are clear boundaries set for women in the afore-mentioned tents, as well as the buildings and tents within prescribed limits. As a result, women are not allowed to leave this space unless for urgent matters and after obtaining permission from a male relative. These women remain surrounded by other women of the same culture or background, despite the fact that they live in a camp that houses a diverse ranges of families, with women from different areas and/or cultural backgrounds. Women are not offered the opportunity to so-cialise and get to know other women outside a particular group of cul-tures nor to spend time and take part in social activities with them in-side the camp. These differences vary based on the areas from which the women come. Although families living in the camp share both na-tionality and religion, their differences include accent, dress, marriage-able age and women's degree of mobility outside the house. Families from certain areas have limited knowledge about the customs and traditions of other areas and shroud them in much stereotyping and prejudice. For instance, according to Bayada customs and traditions, it is preferable for women not to interact with strangers, and they are required to spend time with the women and children of their family. Fear of difference and limited knowledge of the other create more in-centives to reduce interaction with strangers, just as fear of angering the men, and out of adherence to social customs, women from these areas restrict their social relationships to the confines of the family and do not cross the set boundaries. If relationships emerge with other families, they are much weaker than the bonds within the same family. The farther away the female friend's tent is, the more difficult it is to maintain a relationship with her, as both parties need to stay near their house most of the time. This is the case of a girl living in tent (A), who cannot visit her friend in a tent at the centre of the camp because her brother does not allow it. His reasons for not allowing his sister to visit her friend correspond to the ones mentioned above. Such visits are only permitted on very rare occasions, and they are generally short and require permission from male family members.

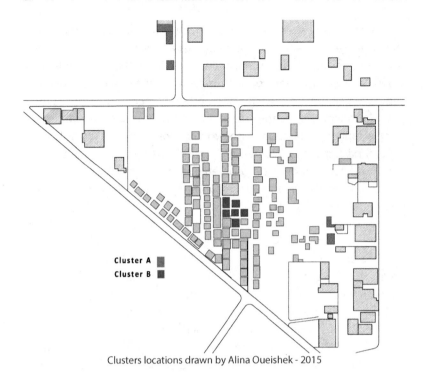

Clusters locations drawn by Alina Oueishek - 2015

2 – Cluster B

Cluster (B) is located at the heart of the camp, including tent (B) and several neighbouring tents. It might be hard for an outsider to pin-point the physical and visible components of this cluster, since its tents are located in the middle of the camp and are adjacent to each other and to surrounding tents. However, the picture becomes clearer after understanding the relationship between the families, and how this relationship manifests itself in simple details in the physicality of the structures.

The house of family (B)'s relatives is located on private land near tent (B) and is built out of blocks and a wooden section, with a ceiling made out of covers. (B)'s relatives purchased the land, built the house on it and invited (B)'s father and mother to come live with them, fol-lowing the deterioration of the situation in their place of residence. The parents were offered to live next-door on a plot of land they were able to obtain rent-free. An additional feature of this cluster is the proximity of the tents inhabited by six families, whose women have been able to develop friendships due to the limited space separating the tents.

These women come from different backgrounds and are of different ages, but they share many similarities and seem to be united in the shared space they live in. During their free time after finishing domestic chores, they exchange social visits between the six tents in the cluster. They often choose tent (H) for their gatherings, as its resident lives alone with her children because her husband works in Beirut and is absent almost the entire month. As a result, her tent is the perfect place for the ladies to meet without having men around. They can spend their time socialising and chit-chatting, without having to worry about the constraints imposed by the presence of men.

Thin walls and light building materials also facilitate communication between neighbouring families, allowing them to talk to one another without having to leave their tents. Several times, the researchers observed one woman invite her neighbour over or ask her to borrow something just by standing and speaking in a slightly raised voice by the wall that is closest to the neighbour's tent. These thin partitions, in addition to the fact that tents are contiguous and pathways are narrow, have a deep impact on family or neighbourly relationships, at times even imposing mandatory interactions. Tent (B), for example, has two entrances, and family members have to take the long way around the entrance of a neighbouring tent during winter, as the main road is often muddy and difficult to cross. During summer, family members take to the main road after it dries out. This mandatory turn puts both families in permanent contact. As a result, and in part due to social courtesy, these bonds between families were strengthened and have led to a sort of friendship. This friendship started out as a result of financial circumstances and social courtesy, and it lasted out of politeness and the ongoing need to have strong relationships with neighbours in order to trade favours and ensure community protection around tents. At times, this friendship becomes uncomfortable for both parties due to the closeness imposed by the positioning of the tents, as well as to the difficulty in having absolute privacy from the surrounding tents.

Women remain close to their tents for different and important reasons: not only do they do so because their husbands or male relatives forbid them from going far, but also because it remains easy to go back and forth if needed. In fact, women's social activities are often interrupted by a demand from their husbands or by the need to check on a sleeping baby in the tent. As such, staying close-by makes it easier for female residents to perform these duties. It also allows them to spend their day freely without much objection from the men, since they remain close to their tents and within a closed and more private women's space. Naturally, the contiguity of the tents contributes greatly to increased contact between women of different backgrounds.

In cluster (B), the researchers have observed friendships between women from different cultures and backgrounds. Women in this cluster are between the ages of fifteen and late thirties, and their children live with them. They come from various areas, including cities like Aleppo and Homs, as well as rural areas like Shebaa and Daraya. The level of participation and independence that these women enjoy, as well as the nature of their relationship with men, with their homes and with their families, vary between these areas. Some women got married at the age of fourteen and did not pursue their education, while others have finished their education. Some of the girls aspire to work and they receive vocational training that increases their level of participation in the community. They also share their experiences with the women who did not have the chance to do so due to the customs of their respective hometowns and families. This type of relationship allows women to become more open, to learn new things and to support each other. In a social gathering, some women were complaining about their husbands beating them and discussing their marital problems. One of them had been married at a young age and divorced her abusive husband. Her presence offered great support to the others, particularly because she was now much stronger and because her relationship with her new husband was different, so she was able to tell her story to other women. This narrative provided unwavering support for the other women in the room who were going through tough times. While several other women at the gathering were being abused and accepted this without turning to their families, due to how common it was for husbands to abuse their wives, this woman in particular enjoyed the support of her father. Her experience, which was unheard of for many women, broadened their horizons in a way. The ability of a woman to get a divorce if she wishes, with her family's support, and to then get remarried, varies from one region to another. In some areas it is very difficult or even practically impossible for women to do so.

3 – General Conclusions

The following section explains how refugees deal with and move around in various spaces within the camp based on their respective roles and needs, as well as on the way they identify with these spaces. Although the camp appears to be one mass of areas and spaces, it is in fact split into clusters and areas within almost invisible borders. These borders are often determined by the refugees' social relationships and roles. Men and children remain in control of public spaces, and one can see men walking around the camp during the day without any constraints, whereas this is not the case for women, who are far more affected by these invisible limitations. In fact, women's areas of mobility are clearly demarcated, mostly based on the distance from their own tents, in accordance with their family's culture or social perceptions. As mentioned above, the role of women in the camp is essentially reproductive (i.e. caring for their children, husbands and homes). The relevant tasks extend over the day and consist of cleaning, preparing food, taking care of infants and being present in the tent when the husband returns during the day to prepare his meal, make him tea, etc. In addition to the fact that men generally keep a close watch on their wives and homes, these tasks constitute additional reasons for the women to remain close to their tents most of the time.

When clusters are located within congested areas of the camp and are surrounded by families from different cultural backgrounds, there is often a positive impact for women, as this increased interaction affords them the opportunity to open up to new cultures and to learn and acquire new ideas or knowledge. Women's experiences with society and family vary between the different cities and rural areas. Their privileges and positions within the family and in society also differ, in addition to the different experiences of women from various generations and those of educated and uneducated women who work in agriculture. By contrast, when the clusters are composed of family members or of people from the same town/city, it tends to have a rather negative impact on women, as they are forced to remain within the same community, unable to socialise with those living outside of these clusters. Daily preoccupations also force women to spend the majority of their time in the tent, and therefore men exert a monopoly on building new relationships. These two factors limit women's ability to spend time away from their tents and to socialise. When there is no case of necessity (e.g. a job inside the camp), these reasons take precedence and are enforced as rules.

Families try to control the peripheries of their cluster by placing additional barriers on the side of unwanted tents, such as rope lines that make it difficult to pass, closing pathways to the tents they do not want to mingle with. This was observed in the case of a family that did not want to socialise with the occupants of a neighbouring tent. In order to avoid contact, they hung a rope to partially block the pathway between the two tents. Neither side wished to socialise with the other, as they came from different areas and did not know each other nor the customs and traditions of their neighbours very well. Each of the two tents has a group of surrounding tents where family members live and with whom they can interact, while at the same isolating themselves from their neighbours through the addition of certain details. This may be done by sectioning off certain parts of the balcony with sheets, blocking the view from the direction of the unwanted family. Balconies are more than just a private space to host visitors, and closing them off from certain directions determines who can or cannot pass by or spontaneously join social gatherings on the balcony.

The researchers also noticed that relationships between clusters are affected by several common factors, as well as by unique circumstances found in each community. Together, however, all clusters constitute one single architectural and social space. Similarly, the areas outside the camp and its peripheries are also characterised by different relationship or management systems. The architecture and nature of the camp's spaces also play a pivotal role in shaping the relationship between the camp and its surroundings, as discussed in the section below.

Forth – The Camp and the Periphery

In most families targeted by the field study, the researchers found that women are more attached to the tent they live in, much as they were to their homes in Syria, keeping in mind that they are seldom allowed to leave without permission from their husbands or male relatives. However, female family members are responsible for preparing food and providing other household needs, in addition to going to relief centres and various organisations to bring the family's share of aid supplies. Therefore, women's mobility, both inside and outside the camp, is often restricted to going to purchase necessary goods. As for the friendships that develop between women, they are usually confined to a perimeter of three or four tents away from their own tents. Consequently, women tend to stay within a small radius in which it is permissible for them to move without being chastised by their male relatives. Even within the confines of this perimeter, women remain close to their tents, so they can easily return there when the children or men need them.

Women who are employed break these constraints to a large extent, as they spend long periods of time outside their homes and assume economic and social roles, without being accompanied by men. As a result, these women are able to communicate with more diverse range of individuals than the ones they get to meet within the confines of their tent. Given that a large number of men at the camps are unemployed, families are often forced to allow female members of the household to be employed. In the case of family (B), girls are able to move with less restrictions within the camp, as they take part in first aid sessions and are members of a local committee in charge of monitoring needs and wants within the camp. The creation of female spaces has also allowed them to leave their homes more frequently. For example, the recently established bakery has become a space that allows women to meet outside their homes. All workers at the bakery are women, and they control who is and is not allowed to enter. This provides them with a private space where they can work, talk and sit as they please, without the scrutiny of intrusive men.

The bakery opens at three in the morning. Women begin their work by preparing the dough, baking it and dividing into loaves that are kept in covered bowls until fermented. A few hours later, the loaves are spread out on boards, baked in the flatbread oven and divided into portions in bags. This process begins from the early morning and lasts roughly until noon. During this time, women go back and forth between their tents and the bakery, depending on their role in the process or their need to be at home with their children. Hence, this proves the importance of creating a female space that motivates female residents to leave their tents and to socialise with other women outside their regular radius of mobility. Although women who work at the bakery live in nearby tents, the space affords them the opportunity to interact with more women from other parts of the camp and improves their mobility and access to outside spaces.

The imposed presence of men, who frequent the bakery to check on the work or to buy goods, is a double-edged sword, since it restricts women's mobility and their capacity to talk freely, while also allowing for socialisation between female and male residents of the camp within common public spaces.

Children under the age of seven or eight spend their entire day close to their mothers. If not enrolled at school, boys over the age of seven or eight spend most of their time in outdoor public spaces within the camp, while girls at that age continue to stay close to their mothers. These girls never leave their homes, especially with the community's heightened sensitivity towards interaction between boys and girls. Although mothers try to control their children's movement within the camp and prefer that they stay close to their tents, the fact that women are always inside makes it difficult to do so. Furthermore, with the strong dominance of male family members prevalent in Syrian society, children tend to obey their fathers more, and mothers usually have to wait for the men to come home to discipline disobedient children. When it comes to young girls, however, the authority of the father is added to social customs imposing limits on their mobility outside their homes, limits that girls are not allowed to cross without the permission of senior family members.

The relationship of female camp residents with the outside world remains weak, as their activity generally consists of shopping trips to provide family needs or of visits to relief or service centres, in particular UNHCR. Women sometimes visit nearby shops or pharmacies, if they need to, but come straight back to the camp. For this reason, the

Monday market represents the sole breathing space, so to speak, for women outside the camp. It is worth noting that single women rarely visit the market alone, as this would be culturally inappropriate, which is why they gather themselves and go in larger groups. This market is an important space for them to meet and chat. They spend their entire Mondays there, right from when the market opens until it closes, buying vegetables and other food and household items they need for the coming week. At night, they return to their tents, carrying heavy bags. Children often wait for their mothers impatiently to return, knowing that they will get their own share of toys and gifts as a result of their mothers' shopping excursion.

Some parents have enrolled their children at the Al Jarahiya camp school. As for children who have yet to reach school age, they go to a centre managed by a fellow camp resident which provides some education and offers a range of recreational activities. When the school day is over, children return to their tents and spend the rest of the day with their mothers or play outside. The children's activity centre is a very important space at the camp, and that is why *Syrian Eyes* has recently increased the amount of activities it organises. The organisation plans to have a weekly play prepared by the children themselves. Through such activities, this centre greatly contributes to children's education and wellbeing, as it provides an alternative to begging, child labour or even just wandering around in the camp without having any engagement or stimulation. Since it is run by individuals from inside and outside the camp who enjoy the trust of camp residents, the centre creates a space where girls can spend time with boys while engaging in different activities. This increases the number of public spaces in the camp, allowing girls to leave their tents in order to socialise, play with and learn from other children in the camp.

Syrian Eyes has had an undeniable role in creating spaces for interaction between residents. The organisation has secured a strong presence at the camp, notably through communication with families and individuals and the wide range of activities and projects it has offered based on the needs of the residents. According to one staff member, camp residents were uncomfortable about the idea of socialising with people from outside the camp at first. However, as members of the organisation began to visit the camp more often and to work with residents on camp improvement projects, the residents became more accepting of outsiders and of those who may be culturally different. By 'different' we mean individuals from different parts of Syria, as well as non-Syrians with whom camp residents had not previously socialised and about whom they had stereotypes and/or preconceived ideas. Another benefit of establishing the centre inside the camp was making it an integral part of the camp, easily accessible by residents without ever having to leave the camp. More specifically, children and women have been allowed benefit from this centre and enter the public space without leaving camp limits and without clashing with social customs and traditions.

Conclusion

This study has presented an overview of the architectural environment of the camp by attempting to answer a central question: how do refugees shape their architectural environment, and what issues or dynamics arise from this process? The study has also sought to identify the role of refugees in building their own, new architectural space, by taking the Al Jarahiya camp in West Bekaa as a case study and looking at how this environment impacts camp residents and influences their lives. The study was structured around a physical description of the camp and its periphery, offering insight on the camp's management system and the relationships established between its residents through the manipulation of borders and the formation of tent clusters.

Among the primary findings of the study was the fact that the legal conditions in Lebanon (the Lebanese government's failure to sign the Convention Relating to the Status of Refugees and to provide housing and basic needs for refugees) and the working methods of NGOs and INGOs in camps have led refugees to assume, by themselves, the task of building and adapting their tents to the physical and social requirements of their lives. Although this mechanism allows refugee families to build their tents in ways that suit them in terms of space distribution, linking tents together and shaping the relationship with their neighbours, these tents remain physically vulnerable and do not provide the necessary degree of protection. This situation stems mostly from the unspoken laws on building materials and how to use them, in addition to the insufficient provision of such materials. This was evident in the fire that engulfed the camp in June 2015 and how the refugees rebuilt their tents after some NGOs supplied them with the necessary raw materials. The fire erupted after a propane cylinder blew up in a tent in at centre of the camp, and it spread very quickly due to the extreme proximity of the tents and the flammability of the tent building materials. In a very short period of time, the flames had torn through the majority of the camp. Only the farthest tents from the centre were spared, including tent (A), which was featured in the study. The other tent examined in the study was completely burned down.

Three families left the camp after the fire, while others took it as an opportunity to expand the size of their tents. None of the families, however, changed the location of their tent; they all maintained the old distributions and relationships with the surrounding tents. The adjustments were limited to increasing the area of the rooms in some cases or adding an extra room and separating the bedroom from the living room, as in the case of tent (B). This demonstrates the stability of the relationships between the residents of the camp, as the separations and connections between their tents were replicated.

During the research process, we observed how balconies act as a divider between the tent's public and private spaces, separating the privacy and sanctity of the tent from the external space, especially given that the materials used for building the tent do not ensure the required level of privacy for the family and only provide a visual barrier from the outside world. Thus, families rely on pre-existing or pre-established safety nets with the neighbouring tents. These relationships are reflected through the orientation of the tent's doors, the fences surrounding the balconies and sometimes even the layout of clothes lines.

It is also important, based on our observations, to stress on the fact that women and children can benefit from activity centres and projects established inside the camp, much more so than from those offered outside the camp, since women's mobility is restricted by customs, traditions and their house-centric role. Despite women's increasing mobility within refugee communities who have been forced to accept women's employment and education in the absence of men or due to men's inability to provide for the family, these constraints continue to exist. Therefore, having activity centres in close proximity to the tents allows women to access public spaces without breaking these constraints entirely. Furthermore, the availability of activity centres and a school for children inside the camp allows parents to be acquainted with the male/female workers, thus earning their trust and making them more willing to benefit from these services and to enrol their children in these facilities. This is of even greater importance in the case of girls, who experience harsher constraints on their mobility due to custom and tradition, not to mention the odd fear for their safety and honour.

It is the researcher's hope that this work will contribute to a better understanding of the aspects of refugee life and culture within the camp, and that it will supplement future research on this topic. Despite the importance and relevance of culture and norms within refugee camps, not much research has been conducted on the subject. While several organisations are implementing projects aimed at supporting or empowering refugee communities, it is counterproductive to brush aside the culture of the groups targeted by these projects. Physical and social considerations are key factors to bear in mind during interventions, in order to improve living standards within the camps and maximise the positive impact of the intervention, while at the same time respecting existing social structures.

It is our belief that in order to ensure enabling environments for work and production, it is critical to be aware of the capacities and preoccupations of targeted communities, in addition to understanding their customs, traditions and needs. These strategies can be combined within an integrated approach to build a socially adequate environment that empowers communities, without causing shocks or imposing ways of living that are alien to these communities.

Sources and References

Bachelard G, *The Poetics of Space*, translated from the French by Maria Jolas, Beacon Press, Boston, 1994.

David H, *The Condition of Post modernity*, Blackwell Publishers, Oxford, 1992.

Dalal A, *Camp Cities between Planning and Practice, Mapping the Urbanization of Zaatari Camp*, Ain Shams University Egypt, University of Stuttgart, Germany, 2014.

Goonewardena, Kipfer, Milgrom, Schmid, *Space, Difference, Everyday Life*, Routledge, New York and London, 2008.

Hillier and Hanson, *The Social Logic of Space*, Cambridge, 1984.

Lefebvre H, *The Production of Space*, translated by Donald Nicholson Smith, Printed in Great Britain, 1991.

Lynch K, *The Image of the City*, Massachusetts Institute of Technology, 1991.

UNHCR, *Convention and protocol relating to the status of refugees*, Communications and Public Information Service

UNHCR, *Promoting Livelihoods and Self-Reliance*, 2011

Electronic References

Jasmin HiLife https://www.jasminhilfe.com/

Jusoor Syria http://jusoorsyria.com/ar./

Save the Children https://www.savethechildren.org/

Sawagroup http://www.sawagroup.org/sg/index.php

Syrian Eyes http://www.syrianeyes.org/index.php?lang=ar

UNHCR https://data2.unhcr.org/en/situations/syria#_ga=1.233162206.1346258812.1493142630

World Vision https://www.worldvision.org

Alina Oueishek

A graduate from the Faculty of Architecture at Damascus University, in 2014, Alina Oueishek works as a designer in a design integration company and lives in Beirut. She has previously worked on project coordination and activity documentation with a number of Syrian organisations in Lebanon, in addition to having established a GIS in High Tech in Damascus.

Political Stereotypes
in the Syrian Uprising

Prepared by: Hani Al Telfah
Supervised by: Marianne Njeim
Research conducted in 2015–2016

Summary

This research paper attempts to understand political stereotypes and their impact on social relationships among individuals and groups within Syrian society during the uprising that began in March 2011. It also aims to analyse some examples of political stereotypes by explaining them linguistically and examining their usage and connotations within the context of the Syrian political discourse during the uprising, with the ultimate goal of discovering the marks that these stereotypes have left on social relationships between individuals. The main research question is thus: have these political stereotypes led to the use of violence and to the annihilation of the other?

The paper begins by introducing the concept of 'stereotype' in general, before defining it based on human, social and political sciences. It then traces the evolution of studies tackling the concept of 'stereotype', particularly the ones that have analysed its role in the formation of political opinions in times war and conflict between nations or among individuals and groups within the same nation.

The paper then discusses how a political stereotype is formulated and explains its components and the functions it performs for the individuals or the political authorities that use it, by citing examples of political stereotypes formulated during the Syrian uprising, such as 'loyalist' (منحبكجي), 'infiltrator' (مندس), 'grey' (رمادي) and 'pro-Assad thug' (شبيح). These images will be studied, deconstructed and linguistically explained in order to determine the contexts in which they are used within the Syrian political discourse and to shed light on their connotations. The research will also rely on the methodologies of political discourse analysis and will provide examples of how the media uses such images.

Additionally, the research paper documents some instances where stereotypes were employed either in political slogans used by political parties or in songs and cartoons used to show support for a certain political position. A random sample of people was also surveyed in order to measure public opinion about the four selected stereotypes, by asking responders to give five descriptions of these stereotypes. The findings summarise the components and characteristics of the selected stereotypes based on the answers of the targeted sample, which comprises around 100 randomly-chosen people.

At the end, the paper attempts to answer the following questions: what are the implications of these stereotypes? Have these stereotypes fuelled the on-going violence in Syria in the past few years? Have they served as tools for each party to the conflict to demonise and dehumanise the other and to justify violence against them? To answer these questions, a number of cases where stereotypes of the 'other' have instigated acts of violence have been examined.

Introduction

People have always resorted to stereotypes as a tool to classify or label 'others', in a way that is similar to basic classification, which helps to simplify and arrange information. Stereotypes are used to store or identify required information without necessarily relying on experience or trying to obtain this information from genuine or objective resources. They also often serve as a cognitive method or mechanism to understand the 'other' and to identify their respective traits.

The Glossary of Media Terms defines a stereotype as "a rigid model or idea that in turn consists of a set of specific and exaggerated assumptions about a certain issue. Such fixed idea is hard to modify, even if evidence to the contrary is presented. A person draws their stereotyped beliefs from their reference group."[1]

Stereotyping is not limited to individual acts or ideas. Rather, it has been incorporated and appropriated by social, religious, political and cultural institutions, and has been utilised for a very particular purpose. Oftentimes, stereotyping is used to influence public opinion or construct a particular image about a defined 'other' for broader aims. Regardless of whether such stereotypes reflect a positive or negative image about the stereotyped group, they remain unrealistic, prejudicial and superficial. The reason behind that is the fact that stereotypes reduce the 'other' to pre-defined and limited characteristics, mostly based on biased sources, rather than on first-hand personal experience, research or knowledge.

Stereotypes emerge in different contexts and are expressed through various mediums. Within varying political and religious contexts, stereotypes are expressed through caricatures, popular jokes and anecdotes, as well as in media and cinema, etc. They seek to shape people's perception of the 'other' (whether this 'other' is groups, people, professions or individuals) based on gender, age or religious, cultural, racial and ethnic affiliations. Stereotypes are likely to emerge, stronger and more defined than before, in times of social conflict or

---

[1] Al Badawi, Ahmad Zaki, *Glossary of Media Terms*, Dar Al Kitab Al Masri, Cairo, 1985, p 145.

war, when there is a need to demonise the 'other' or ascribe to them all sorts of traits with the intent of delegitimising them, thus securing gains or credibility in the conflict.

This research aims to analyse the components and trends of political stereotyping which have emerged in Syrian political discourse since 2011, by identifying the features of popular or prevalent stereotypes among the segments of Syrian society today. This paper will also focus on the following manifestations of political stereotyping: loyalist (منحبكجي/ة)—infiltrator (مندس/ة)—"grey" (رمادي/ة)—"Shabih" or pro-Assad thug (شبيح/ة). The paper will explore the linguistic sources of these specific manifestations and try to further dissect them in order to better understand how they correlate with the broader social, cultural or political context.

The aim of this paper is to examine certain political stereotypes that have emerged or have been defined during the Syrian uprising, as well as to analyse their use in Syrian political discourses, in order to determine the extent of their negative impact on social relations within the country. The paper also raises the following questions: have these stereotypes harmed social relations among the individuals and groups of Syrian society? Do they inspire or provoke violence and condone the exclusion or eradication of the 'other'?

First, it is important to introduce and define what a stereotype is in general, before presenting several definitions of the term as described in sociology and social sciences, in order to reach an accurate and concise definition. At the next stage, the paper will examine political stereotypes in general, using quantitative and qualitative analyses drawing on the findings of online questionnaires targeting a random sample of 100 Syrians as respondents. The purpose of this survey was to examine the characteristics of certain political stereotypes in order to give nuance to and shed light on the research conducted on these stereotypes. Finally, the paper will analyse the negative impact of these stereotypes on social relations among individuals and groups within Syrian society.

During the course of the research, certain difficulties were encountered, including insufficient reference material in Arabic, whether cultural or sociological, as most available references were non-Arabic and not translated into Arabic. Therefore, the research was confined to a single analysis model, resulting in reference gaps. This particularly applies to relaying the research in an Arabic context. For this reason, stereotypes are explained from a linguistic perspective and their linguistic connotations are examined in order to compare them to the connotations provided by the respondents.

Ultimately, it is the aim of this research to take a step further towards analysing the political stereotypes that emerged during the Syrian uprising and providing a theoretical framework to overcome the negative consequences of their wide-scale use in the media, in political discourse or in the daily lives and imagination of Syrians.

First – The Stereotype

This section introduces the concept of 'stereotype' by presenting various definitions of the term from different branches of knowledge, with particular focus on its use in sociological or psychological studies, in order to form a general picture about what the concept of 'stereotype' refers to. Subsequently, we will trace the stages of development of stereotypes, in order to eventually understand them through their formation mechanism: what are the elements or dynamics that shape the stereotype in general? What is the impact of stereotypes on broader social relations?

1 – Introduction to the Concept of Stereotype

The concept of stereotype appeared in various fields of research and became widely used, especially in contemporary and modern social research. The topic of stereotypes also gained popularity in media studies at all levels, as well as in politics, psychology, sociology and academia.

US journalist and researcher Walter Lippmann (1889–1974) was among the first to introduce the concept of stereotype in his 1922 book entitled *Public Opinion*. In this book, Lippmann attempted to examine US public opinion in the wake of the First World War, particularly how public opinion was formed and the factors that influenced it. The second chapter of the book, entitled "The Stereotype", provides the following definition: "The only feeling that anyone can have about an event he does not experience is the feeling aroused by his mental image of that event. We shall assume that what each man does is based not on direct and certain knowledge, but on pictures made by him or given to him."[2]

Lippmann goes on to explain that the individual assumes that he/she knows the world and gives value judgments about a general event or issue, despite not really having enough experience or knowledge to make such judgments on these topics or issues. The in-

---

[2]   Lippmann. Walter, *Public opinion*, Harcort, Brace Company, New York, 1922, p 90–91.

dividual then adopts certain judgments as a result of the stereotype he/she has already formed in order to have a preconception of his/her community and world.[3] According to Lippmann, stereotyping, or the formation of stereotypes by individuals, may in fact be a defence mechanism adopted by an individual to ensure a sort of self-protection or to protect their group. Stereotyping is not only practiced by individuals but also by groups and societies on a wider scale.[4]

Following in Lippmann's footsteps, interest in the concept of stereotype increased among sociologists and media experts, particularly after the Second World War, during which stereotypes based on race or ethnicity were widely used. The notion of stereotyping was also introduced to behavioural studies as part of the effort to understand collective behaviour. In other words, stereotypes referred to common features ascribed to people from a certain nationality, for example, by people from another nationality. The common belief in static features of the 'other' is formulated on unscientific and non-objective grounds, generally under the influence of bigoted ideas marked by a standardised or oversimplified perception of the 'other'. Such ideas are normally inspired by current political discourse as well as advertising and media.

Moreover, psychologists discussed and analysed the notion of the stereotype extensively, which allowed them to better understand the relationship between the individual and his/her environment or community. The impact of the stereotype on the attitudes and behaviours of the individual was also analysed, as well as their ability to cope with his/her community in light of such stereotypes. US psychologist Gordon Allport (1897–1967) explained the significance of stereotyping practiced by the individual as one of the main indicators that reflect social and cultural trends among individuals.[5]

As for political science, specialists in this field have studied the impact of the stereotype on internal and external political decision-making. This relates to both the effect of political relations on individ-

---

[3]   For further information, please refer to the following reference: Lippmann. Walter, *Public opinion*, op.cit., p 93–94.
[4]   For further information, please refer to the following reference: Lippmann. Walter, *Public opinion*, op.cit., p 93–94.
[5]   Sulayman, Salih, *The Media and the Production of Stereotypes*, Al Falah Library For Publishing & Distribution, Kuwait, 2005, p 144.

uals and groups from the same community on the one hand, and to international relations between countries on the other hand. These studies have attempted to highlight the role of the stereotype in violent and non-violent conflicts, both inside and outside the borders of a country or society.[6]

The notion or idea of the stereotype has evolved since the 1920s and still shapes the opinions of individuals to this day, spreading into various fields of knowledge, such as philosophy, psychology, ethnology, politics, sociology, media, gender, linguistics, literature, arts and many others. Bearing that in mind, it is difficult to establish a comprehensive definition of the stereotype in its modern sense, due to the huge discrepancies between various disciplines. Therefore, this paper will present a range of definitions of the stereotype from the fields of psychology and sociology, in an attempt to reach a clearer understanding of the concept and its usage.

2 – Definitions of the Stereotype

There is no standardised definition of the stereotype used by sociologists and psychologists. Multiple definitions have emerged and have been changed or adapted according to the field of study. In this section, we will present the most prominent definitions, relying on linguistics and the root or source of a word of concept, as well as on social sciences and psychology, in order to reach a relevant definition that will be used as reference in subsequent parts of the study.

When it comes to linguistics and etymology, the term "stereotype" has no single Arabic equivalent. Therefore, we will use the term "الصورة النمطية", which was employed by the first scholars who addressed this topic, such as Edmund Ghareeb, Hisham Sharabi, Edward Sa'id, Mikha'il Sulayman and others.[7] The *Oxford Dictionary* and the *International Encyclopedia of the Social Sciences* give the following definition to the term "stereotype": "The method or process of printing, whereby a printing surface is used to produce thousands of identical copies of a message, and the printing process is repeated mechanically without

---

[6]   Iradat Al Jabouri, *Conferences on the Stereotype*, Faculty of Media, University of Baghdad, [s.n], [n.d], p 14.
[7]   Iradat Al Jabouri, *Conferences on the Stereotype*, Faculty of Media, University of Baghdad, [n.s], [s.d], p 12.

the need to form a new mould."[8] The term "stereotype", in its sociological and psychological sense, was inspired by this specific use of mass printing and metal moulds. One can benefit from this "technological" definition to identify some features of the concept of stereotype, as these latter are repeatedly used, exchanged and spread on a wide scale among individuals and groups in society.

Within the social context, one finds the definition put forward by US journalist and researcher Walter Lippmann, who, as mentioned before, was among the first scholars to approach the concept of the stereotype in his book *Public Opinion*, published in 1922. In his work, he defined the stereotype as "a regular and abridged process of depicting the world, societies and the others in a manner that reflects one's values and beliefs."[9]

In 1993, sociologist Preston Dyer (1969) defined the term as follows: "a regular process: stereotypes are used to give meaning to society by way of generalisation and application of patterns. Therefore, people carry out this process on a regular basis. The stereotype is abridged: it is an easy method to present complicated information. Reducing a certain group or nation to a repeated stereotype restricts the scope of knowledge whereby a person views such group or people".

The stereotype deciphers the world: it helps the person understand his/her immediate surroundings and determines their perception of community and society. However, based on the aforementioned definitions, one cannot help but wonder what version of the world is depicted by the stereotype. There is, no doubt, a vast difference between reality and its abridged version reflected by the stereotype. Therefore, the stereotype only provides a superficial knowledge of others. It reflects (or deflects) values: it is an influential means of gathering consensus around a public perception of a group or category of people. In other words, it is a general agreement among a group of individuals.[10]

---

[8] Definition from the *Dictionary of the Social Sciences – Oxford*, [online reference], Oxford website, http//goo.gl/qLyBYr, [s.d.], reviewed on 12/7/2016.

[9] For further information, please refer to: Lippmann. Walter, *Public opinion*, op.cit., p 81.

[10] Preston Dyer, *The matter of the images: essays on representations*, London: Routledge, 1993, p 63–69.

As for the definition of "stereotype" in the field of psychology as articulated in the *Encyclopaedia of Psychology* issued by the Arab Institute for Research and Publishing, it is "the idea that is increasingly repeated in the same rigid manner called pattern, which refers to the mental image commonly adopted by certain individuals or groups."[11]

Based on the aforementioned definitions, one can make the following observations:

- The stereotype is a cognitive construct that encompasses one's own knowledge, beliefs and expectations regarding a social group;
- The stereotype is an oversimplified idea linking behavioural characteristics to a specific group;
- The stereotype is a set of beliefs regarding the characteristics of a specific group. It is used in an automatic and subconscious manner;

In light of these definitions, it is clear that many psychologists agree that the stereotype is a cognitive construct (cognitive structure) that involves expectations about a specific group, influencing one's attitude towards the stereotyped group and one's handling of the information collected about this group.

Based on the above, it is possible to define the stereotype as a positive or negative value judgment related to a specific category of people (racial, religious, gender-based, or politically-affiliated). This judgment is made with no consideration of objectivity or personal experience and is irrespective of individual differences between the members of that group. In fact, it binds them all to a single picture, feature or myth that is often difficult to change. Stereotypes might be social, racial or political.

Within the Syrian context, the stereotype represents a main feature of the political discourse as expressed in social media, whether official or unofficial. The reciprocal use of stereotypes has magnified political polarisation in the country, deepened fear of the 'other' and widened socio-political disparities. Examples on such cases abound and vary

---

[11]   Marzouk, Asaad, *Encyclopaedia* of *Psychology*, Arab Institute for Research and Publishing, Beirut, 1987, p 320.

from one period to another. Therefore, it was necessary to present an extended definition of the political stereotype in general, tackling its utility, components and content, before analysing a series of examples that emerged in Syria during the uprising.

Second – The Political Stereotype

In this section, the paper will address stereotypes more extensively and examine their use or presence in political texts as part of the broader political discourse. The paper will also explore the motivations behind the use of stereotypes by political figures or leaders through various examples on such cases. This will serve to explain how certain stereotypes were formed, what their components are and where and how they are used, in order to illustrate their broader effects on society and politics.

1 – The Stereotype in the Political Text

The political text is a part of the political discourse or a component thereof. According to British linguistics researcher Norman Fairclough (1941), author of the book *Language and Power*, the discourse is a medium to understand the world around us and the social structure. The discourse consists of the three following elements:

1) The text, which includes written or spoken text, pictures, movies and any other means whereby ideas are communicated.
2) The practice that accompanies the discourse, such as the place where the discourse is given.
3) The social structure, which can impact the discourse and the receiver.[12]

This paper will address the first element of discourse, which is the text, without addressing or delving into the remaining two elements, as they are not directly related to the focus of this paper.

In his book *Public Opinion*, Lippmann describes the emergence of stereotypes within the framework of the political text and propaganda practiced by media outlets in particular, which is one instance of the political discourses that represent diversified political opinions.[13] In fact, stereotypes appeared in the political text before the concept of stereotype was explicitly defined. Lippmann explains that political ste-

---

[12] Fairclough, Norman, *Discourse as Social Practice*, op.cit., p 156.
[13] Lippmann. Walter, *Public opinion*, op.cit., p 50–56.

reotypes appeared in the political texts of countries fighting against Germany in the First World War in order to describe German soldiers. These stereotypes portrayed the German soldier as being violent, corrupt and inhuman, almost depicting him as the devil incarnate. German soldiers were also described as being stupid, ignorant and enslaved to their master.[14]

To further elaborate this point, Walter Lippmann states that "Political leaders and ordinary citizens need to be involved in decision-making when it comes to complicated matters they do not understand. Consequently, leaders and citizens rely on the stereotypes that they form based on other sources, excluding direct experience, since one sees what one expects to see rather than what is actually present in reality. Therefore, stereotypes represent one's vision of reality, even if the acquired knowledge stemming from direct experience contradicts the stereotype."[15]

Lippmann observed that these stereotypes are used to ensure certain benefits for the political authority, namely gaining public support for mobilisation in its conflict against other actors or nations. Texts published by the political authority involve generalised and non-objective attributes about an entire group, with the aim of undermining or tarnishing the image of this group in public opinion. This is ensured by ascribing certain attributes to the 'other' using multiple channels, including the media, advertisements, caricatures, etc.

One example of such deformed images of the 'other' is the stereotype promoted by the political authority in the United States against communists during the Cold War, whereby the communist was portrayed as an enemy of questionable morals, often a drunkard who is licentious, impulsive, dictatorial and disrespectful of social traditions. Such stereotypes were featured in the political rhetoric of successive US presidents during the Cold War, as well as in several movies and TV series, and became the object of study in the US.[16]

Such examples illustrate the role and impact of political stereotypes, especially those shaped by political texts reflecting the image of

---

[14]   Lippmann. Walter, *Public opinion*, op.cit., p 40–41.
[15]   Lippmann. Walter, *Public opinion*, op.cit., p 56.
[16]   Please refer to: Moskowitz, Gordon B. *Social Cognition: Understanding Self and Others*, Guilford Press, New York, 2005, p 182.

a political actor. Stereotypes serve to gain public support by forming a rigid and unrealistic image of the other. Therefore, individuals who adopt stereotypes issue value judgments about the 'other', particularly those belonging to rival countries or groups.

By analysing the political text, one can identify the elements and content of political stereotypes and infer their connotations.

2 – Elements and Content of Political Stereotypes

The political stereotype can be briefly defined as the set of attributes scribed to a specific category of individuals and groups, regardless of whether they are positive or negative. The political stereotype is the product of a fantastical and partial perception that is not based on experience. The traits attributed to a stereotyped group differentiate it from other groups, not necessarily in a negative manner. Such differentiation could be positive and subject to change with time.

Social psychologist Susan Fiske (1952) argues that "the attributes and content of stereotypes might be positive. For example, a group of people might be stereotyped as having successful social relations or respecting the value of security or being non-violent."[17] Fiske also points out, in her study on stereotypes, that even if the stereotypes concerning a group of people are positive, this does not necessarily mean that they are true. The qualities attributed to people through stereotypes are, in a way, similar to predictive studies, whose findings should not be seen as conclusive. Instead, the experimental method should be adopted to that end.[18]

Lippmann indicates that stereotypes can be formed on the basis of a cognitive mechanism known as "the virtual relation", i.e. the wrong conclusion about the relation between two events or topics. This mechanism is activated when there is a lack of information or a state of ambiguity about the matter.[19]

Not only is the stereotype a particular mind-set that carries material or moral qualifications of the 'other', it is also generalised to include all

---

[17] Fiske, Susan, and Cuddy, Amy. *Stereotype Content Model*, Journal of Personality and Social Psychology, 2002 VOL 82, p 878.

[18] Fiske, Susan, and Cuddy, Amy. *Stereotype Content Model*, Op.cit., p 884.

[19] For further information, please refer to the following reference: Lippmann. Walter, *Public opinion*, op.cit., p 93–98.

the components or elements of this 'other'. Its content is also marked by the following characteristics:

1) Reductionist simplification: disregarding the human composition, the reality and events that require deeper analysis;
2) Overwhelming generalisation: disregarding diversity, differences and disparities, without consideration of individual differences or personal traits for example. Such differences, however, need to be taken into account in any reasonable judgement;
3) Rigidity: refusing to change the idea since it contains, in the mind of its holder, value judgments about the stereotyped target, charged with personal emotions that have accumulated over time. However, this rigidity is at odds with reality and does not take into account the changes and dynamics of human groups and societies.[20]

It is worth noting, in this regard, that it is possible for one element of the stereotype to change without radically altering or destroying the stereotype as a whole; although stereotypes may be likened to precast moulds, they can constantly bring in or create new attributes.

In Syria, political stereotypes have played a central role in formulating the discourses of opposing political actors. A wide array of designations and terms have surfaced in official and unofficial social, political and media discourses, which were not solely used by the government/regime and the opposition, but also by the social base that welcomed these new additions to its daily lexicon. In the upcoming section, we will explore the general nature of this new discourse and study specific examples of such terminology.

---

[20] Fiske, Susan, and Cuddy, Amy. *Stereotype Content Model*, Op.cit., 889–902.

Third – The Political Stereotype during the Syrian Uprising

In the first part of this section, we will provide a historical overview of the Syrian uprising, with its major events and watershed moments. In order to explore the context in which political stereotypes were formed, this paper will attempt to highlight the stereotypes that appeared in Syrian political texts during the uprising, reflecting the different emerging political views throughout this period. The paper will also present examples of such stereotypes, explaining their linguistic connotations and meaning, as well as the context in which they were used. The findings of a questionnaire distributed as part of the research will also be presented, in order to pinpoint the traits of the stereotypes found or expressed by respondents. The paper will then explain the negative effects that these stereotypes have on relations between individuals and groups within Syrian society, by giving examples of violent incidents where stereotypes were a motive for committing violence.

1 – Overview of the Syrian Political Uprising

In March 2011, Syria witnessed the beginning of a popular political uprising, marked by peaceful protests across several Syrian cities. These protests were considered part of the so-called Arab Spring that swept over several Arab countries, including Tunisia and Egypt, and featured slogans such as "The people want to bring down the regime", "God, Syria, Freedom and Nothing Else" and "The Syrian people will not be humiliated".[21]

As public demonstrations continued and spread to various cities, the uprising grew and took on other forms of popular engagement, including the distribution of pamphlets, the writing of slogans on walls and an increasing number of demonstrations in major cities. The response of the Syrian authorities was regrettable, as they resorted to

---

[21] Shehayid, Jamal, *Anti-regime and Pro-regime Slogans in Syria*, [online reference], Arab Reform Initiative website, http://goo.gl/YXxAea, January 2012, reviewed on 14-07-2016.

the use of force and cracked down on the demonstrations and protests, leading to a number of casualties and mass arrests of many activists who took part in the uprising.[22]

While public demonstrations continued to expand and Syrian security forces continued their crackdown on the uprising, new political bodies began to emerge, making clear their opposition to the regime that had ruled Syria since 1970. However, the opposition was not the only party active in the public space and holding demonstrations; pro-regime marches were organised and chanted different slogans, such as "With our souls, with our blood, we will sacrifice ourselves for you, O Bashar!", "Syria is protected by God" and "We are your men, Bashar".[23]

The Local Coordination Committees emerged in Syria in 2011 as local organisation bodies and were involved in organising protests, documenting violations and disseminating data to create a new political rhetoric in the country. The Syrian National Transitional Council was later formed in November 2011, and it brought together the majority of opposition parties in Syria. The National Transitional Council remained the major representative body of the Syrian opposition until the end of 2013.[24] Afterwards, several political bodies embraced the position of the Syrian opposition and were represented by the National Coordination Body, the Kurdish National Council and the National Coalition for Syrian Revolution and Opposition Forces.[25] As for the positions towards the political regime in Syria, Syrians were divided among pro-regime, anti-regime and neutral Syrians who did not identify with either political project.

The uprising later turned into an armed conflict between the two opposing parties, particularly after the Free Syrian Army was formed in early 2012 by the officers and soldiers who had defected from the Syrian Arab Army and security services and by volunteers. The Free Syrian Army originally proclaimed that its function was simply to protect pro-

---

[22]   Bishara, Azmi, *Syria: A Path to Freedom from Suffering—An Attempt in Contemporary History, Arab Center for Research and Policy Studies, Beirut, 2013, p 79–85.*

[23]   Shehayid, Jamal, *Anti-regime and Pro-regime Slogans in Syria*, op.cit..

[24]   Bishara, Azmi, *Syria: A Path to Freedom from Suffering—An Attempt in Contemporary History, op.cit., p 404–420.*

[25]   Bishara, Azmi, *Syria: A Path to Freedom from Suffering—An Attempt in Contemporary History, op.cit., p 404–420.*

testors from security services, which had used excessive force against protesters. However, the situation soon turned into a full-scale military confrontation between the FSA and the regular army, escalating into a broad and acute armed conflict.[26]

As mentioned earlier, the use of stereotypes and stereotyping increases during period of conflict and wars. The Syrian uprising was no exception, and Syrian political texts began featuring terms that steadily turned into stereotypes about the 'other' on the opposite side of the political spectrum.

2 – The Syrian Political Text and Stereotypes

Political actors on both sides of the spectrum tried to win over their public or the social base that shared their political opinion. Consequently, political texts criticised and attacked the other's opinion and issued judgments against it. The Syrian regime has used the terms "infiltrator" (المُندس) and "infiltrators" (المدسوسين) since the beginning of the uprising. During the sit-in organised in front of the Ministry of Interior in Damascus on the 16th of March 2011, the Ministry issued a statement about the sit-in in the official gazette to the following effect: "While some parents were submitting written motions about their relatives who were arrested for various crimes, infiltrators tried to exploit the situation and call for protest by raising a number of slogans in order to sow chaos".[27] The official media claimed that infiltrators were placed in the protests to encourage violence against state institutions; these infiltrators were portrayed as "traitors in thrall to foreign countries, who do not hesitate to open fire on civilians and intimidate them by infiltrating the protests".[28] As a matter of fact, the term "infiltrator" could be attributed to any member of the opposition in order to justify

---

[26]   Bishara, Azmi, *Syria: A Path to Freedom from Suffering*—An Attempt in Contemporary History, op.cit., p 196–197.

[27]   *Infiltrators tour security centers and other institutions claiming they have instructions to police members to use violence*, [online reference], Al Thawra Newspaper, http://tinyurl.com/jbb7dbb, 9-04-2011, reviewed on 17-02-2016.

[28]   *Infiltrators tour security centers and other institutions claiming they have instructions to police members to use violence*, [online reference], Al Thawra Newspaper, http://tinyurl.com/jbb7dbb, 9-04-2011, reviewed on 17-02-2016.

their arrest and punishment by security forces due to their political views.

Individuals who supported the regime of Bashar Al Assad were labelled as "loyalists" (المنحبكجي), a term inspired by the 2007 media campaign that was launched during the last referendum of Bashar Al Assad to renew his term as President. The main slogan of the campaign was "We Love You" (منحبك).[29] The term "thugs" (الشبيحة) was also increasingly used in political texts by members of the opposition to refer to individuals who joined pro-regime security bodies and parties,[30] as well as to describe those who defended the ruling regime in the media and in the cultural and social circles of Syrian society.[31] As for the individuals who had a neutral stance towards the conflict, they were described as "the grey" (رمادي) so as to reflect their political position that neither opposed nor backed the Syrian regime; neither black nor white.

Based on the above, one can notice that individuals of Syrian society were categorised according to their political views as either "infiltrators", "loyalists", "greys" or "thugs". Stereotyping might be an act of categorisation at first, but it can quickly turn into a mould in which individuals are placed by way of repetition. Based on the aforementioned components of stereotypes their sociological definition as abridged versions of reality reflecting the values and views of the person issuing them, we will attempt, in the section below, to determine the elements, features and contents of the following stereotypes by studying each of them separately: "infiltrator", "loyalist", "thug" and "grey". We will also try to determine whether the aforementioned elements of reductionism, generalisation and rigidity apply to these stereotypes.

---

[29] *Presidential campaign turns into an "oath of allegiance" to Assad in Damascus' streets*, [online reference], Al Quds Al Arabi Newspaper website, http://www.alquds.co.uk/?p=166848, 12-05-2014, reviewed on 17-02-2016.

[30] Bishara, Azmi, *Syria: A Path to Freedom from Suffering—An Attempt in Contemporary History, op.cit., p 264–265.*

[31] Bishara, Azmi, *Syria: A Path to Freedom from Suffering—An Attempt in Contemporary History, op.cit., p 266–267.*

3 – Political Stereotypes

In this section, the paper will explore four political stereotypes by presenting their linguistic definition and describing their uses and political connotations. It will also review the results of the questionnaire distributed to 100 participants to sample their opinion with regards to the stereotypes in question. It is worth mentioning that the purposive sampling approach was adopted, as respondents were selected based on their different political views, age and gender.

a – "منحبكجي" (Loyalist)

- Language and etymology: "منحبك" is an Arabic term meaning "we love you". The "جي" suffix, which is used in Syrian slang and is derived from Turkish, indicates one's profession or one's mastery in the verb/skill it is added to. For example, the grocer is called in Arabic "خضرجي" (the one who sells vegetables) and the shoemaker is called "كندرجي" (master of shoes), etc.[32]
- Use and political connotation: the term "منحبك" (We Love You) was the slogan of the referendum campaign of Syrian President Bashar Al Assad in 2007. It appeared on billboards and advertisements, as well as in the electoral propaganda on official TV channels, as well as official and non-official newspapers supporting Bashar Al Assad.[33]

During the Syrian uprising, the term "منحبكجي" was reclaimed by members of the opposition to refer to pro-Assad or pro-regime[34] individuals.

When respondents were asked about the connotations of the term "المنحبكجي/ة", they answered as follows:

---

[32] Shehadeh, Hasib, *Arabic Terms of Turkish Origin*, [online reference], Donia Al Watan Online Newspaper, http://goo.gl/fA5rrp, published on 19-10-2010, reviewed on 7-2-2016.

[33] *The Presidential campaign of Syrian President Bashar Al Assad*, [online reference], Asharq Al Awsat, Issue 10407, http://tinyurl.com/h9zsjow, 27-05-2007, reviewed on 9-01-2016.

[34] Dabbagh, Basim, *Semiology of the Arabic Suffix "Jee" and its derivatives*, [online reference], Al Modon Online Newspaper, http://tinyurl.com/j4v6dy9, published on 22-03-2014, reviewed on 28-01-2016.

Supporter	94%	Emotional	80%	Idiot	63%
Coward	53%	Traditionalist	40%	Faithful	28%
Traitor	17%	Patriotic	9%		

This data shows that the stereotype "المنحبكجي/ة" not only reflects political views, but also implies other traits in a biased manner and insistently reduces the pro-regime individual to such traits. It also contains a value judgment towards this individual, describing him as a traitor or a patriot, without being restricted to the judgement on political views alone.

This stereotype was repeatedly used in opposition discourse and introduced into caricatures mocking the character of the regime supporter. Examples abound in that regard, including the caricature of the Syrian political cartoonist Ali Farzat[35], mocking a person labelled as "منحبكجي 2012 model", whose hands are reflected on the wall as a donkey's ears.

---

[35]   To review the caricatures, please refer to artist Ali Farzat's website: http://www.ali-ferzat.com/.

© Ali Ferzat. Reprinted with kind permission.

Another example is a drawing showing the difference between two artists, one of whom is the pro-regime Duraid Lahham and the other is Yassin Bakoush, an actor known for being Duraid Lahham's comedic partner in his role as "Yasino" in comedy shows. Bakoush died in 2013 after his car was bombed in Damascus. The drawing shows Duraid Lahham receiving a medal from Syrian President Bashar Assad, with the title at the top of the picture describing Duraid Lahham as "المنحبكجي" and the picture featuring fake Syrian stamps, whereas Yassin Bakoush's picture features Syrian Revolution stamps.

95

© Ammar al-Beik: The Martyr And The Traitor. Stamps of The Syrian Revolution[36].
Reprinted with kind permission

Through such uses, one notices that the term "المنحبكجي/ة" reflects the conditions set by Lippmann to the formation of a stereotype, since it reduces individuals and confines them to a certain mould because of their political views. At the same time, it contains a biased value judgement not based on personal experience.

b – "الشَّبِّيحَ/ة" (Thugs)

- Language and etymology: "الشَّبِّيحَة" is a term derived from the verb "شبَح", meaning to commit thuggery.[37] The residents of the

---

[36] This image is taken from the Facebook page entitled "Stamps of The Syrian Revolution", to reach the full collection: https://www.facebook.com/Stamps.of.the.syrian.revolution/

Syrian coastal region use the exaggerated formula "فَعِّيل" instead of the ordinary one "فَعَال" for exaggeration purposes. For example, the term "رِسِّيم" is used to describe a skilled painter ("رسَّام"). Another signification of the term, in both its plural form "شَبِّيحة" and singular form "شَبِّيح", is the ghost beyond imagination. The origin of the term, however, is not clear. One possibility is that it is derived from "أشباح" (ghosts). This does correlate with the connotations of the term "الشَّبِّيحة" (the thugs), who are outlaws working in the dark, both literally and figuratively, and quickly disappearing in an unidentified Mercedes-Benz S without a license plate— a car colloquially known as "الشبح" (the ghost), known to be the trademark car used by leading "thugs" in their operations.[38]

- Use and political connotation: the term entered the Syrian lexicon during the second half of the seventies, following the Syrian intervention in Lebanon in 1976, which was coupled with a drastic increase in smuggling activity from Lebanon, an excessively open country, to the economically closed Syria. The term gained popularity during the Syrian uprising and was used to describe informal militias employed by the regime to counter protesters across the country. With its generalising aspect, the term shifted away from its original signification to describe the pro-regime groups that resort to violence, be it physical or verbal, against anti-regime individuals.[39]

As for its popular usage, the term has appeared in slogans raised during opposition protests and pro-regime marches. This has given the term a dual usage in:

1) Slogans attacking political actors to whom these traits were ascribed. The slogan "شبيحة، شبيحة!" was raised when Syrian security forcibly dispersed protesters in Syrian cities.
2) Slogans chanted by people who embrace the "الشبيحة" trait and take pride in it; a video broadcast on the official Syrian TV shows

---

37 Definiton of the term "رمادي" (gray) in Almaany dictionary, [online reference], Almaany website: http://goo.gl/TWUJec, [s.d], reviewed on 07-17-2016.

38 Al Hajj Salih, Yasin, *On Thugs, Thuggery and their State*, Kalamon magazine, Issue No. 5, Beirut, Winter 2012, p 1

39 Al Hajj Salih, Yasin, *On Thugs, Thuggery and their State*, op.cit., p 2–3.

a crowd gathered at the Umayyad Square in Damascus to hear the Syrian President's speech. Once the speech was over, the crowd chanted the following slogans: "We, the hungry "شبيحة" (thugs), want to eat "المندسين" (the infiltrators)" and ""شبيحة"" (Thugs) forever, for Assad's sake".[40]

In the questionnaire conducted as part of the survey, the respondents answered with the following when asked about the traits they assign to "الشَّبّيح/ة" (thugs):

Violent	95%	Criminal	89%	Thief	82%
Supporter	64%	Huge	54%	Despicable	44%
Apostate	37%	Animal	29%	Psychopath	14%

This data shows that the respondents have stereotyped "الشبيحة" (the thugs) and given them traits related to their faith, character and appearance, assuming in advance acts such as theft and criminality. The respondents have also assumed that the thugs do not believe in God, since the results show that some respondents consider them to be 'apostates' and give them unrealistic and reductive traits that are not solely restricted to their political views, but also encompass their attitude and beliefs and fit them into a single mould or stereotype.

c – "مُندس/ة" (Infiltrators)

- Language and etymology: this term is derived from "الدَّسُّ" (insinuate), which is defined in the Arab dictionary *Lisan Al Arab* as follows: "insert something from underneath". In the *Al Muhit* dictionary, "الدس" (insinuation) is hiding and burying something beneath another and "اندسَ" (infiltrate) is "embedding oneself".[41]
- Use and political connotation: at the beginning, official and semi-official media outlets used the term to insinuate the presence of infiltrators in popular protests and demonstrations who open fire on security forces and protesters in order to sow cha-

---

40   Shehayid, Jamal, *Anti-regime and Pro-regime Slogans in Syria*, op.cit.
41   Definiton of the term "مندس" (infiltrator) in Almaany dictionary, [online reference], Almaany website: http://goo.gl/ZlI2ot, [s.d], reviewed on 07-17-2016.

os, based on the instructions of foreign countries supplying them with funds and equipment.[42]

- The term figured in the data published by the Syrian Ministry of Interior in the official newspaper *Al Thawra* (The Revolution): "Some infiltrated elements tour a number of security centres and other institutions, impersonating security officials and high-ranking officers and claiming that they have strict instructions to police members to use violence and live bullets to target any suspicious gathering".[43]

The term "المندسين" (infiltrators) was also used in the speech of Syrian President Bashar Assad, who indicated the presence of infiltrators or agents inserting themselves into popular protests in order to cause riots and vandalism and attack state property and security forces.[44]

As for the results of the questionnaire, the respondents answered as follows:

Rebel	87%	Opponent	79%	Activist	65%
Protester	54%	Intelligent	30%	Agent	13%
Traitor	7%				

It is worth mentioning that, according to these results, most of the traits ascribed to the stereotype of "المندس/ة" (infiltrator) do not actually reflect the linguistic meaning of the term, since they refer to attributes having to do with politics, so to speak, such as "intelligence". They also imply in advance that the infiltrator participates in protests and undertakes social and/or political activity. Therefore, these traits are not objective and reduce the individual simply to his/her political opinion.

---

[42] Bishara, Azmi, *Syria: A Path to Freedom from Suffering—An Attempt in Contemporary History, op.cit., p 79–85.*

[43] *Infiltrators tour security centers and other institutions claiming they have instructions to police members to use violence,* [online reference], Al Thawra Newspaper website, http://tinyurl.com/jbb7dbb, 21-03-2011, reviewed on 14-02-2016.

[44] *The Speech of President Bashar Al Assad to the People's Council,* [online reference], Réseau Voltaire website, http://goo.gl/v2exAr, published on 30-03-2011, reviewed on 04-02-2016.

d – "رمادي/ة" (Grey)

- Language and etymology: "رَمادِيّ" (grey) is attributed to "رَماد" (ash) or the colour of ash, which lies between black and white and comes both in lighter and darker shades.[45]
- Use and political connotation: the term "رَمادِيّ" (grey) is used to refer to the individuals who do not adopt any political views, neither in support nor against the ruling political regime in Syria. These individuals have been described as "grey" for being "neither black nor white", which are the two colours symbolising the good and evil sides of the conflict. Individuals who not adopt a political position have been criticised by both regime supporters and opposition members.[46] Several pages were created on social media accusing the "greys" of conspiring to wreck the nation and helping the evil side by embracing such a neutral position.

As for the results of the questionnaire (which asked respondents to give the first 5 traits of the "greys"), the respondents answered as follows:

Afraid	93%	Neutral	91%	Hypocrite	85%
Coward	76%	Non-affiliated	61%	Intelligent	58%
Indifferent	40%	Opportunist	36%		

According to these results, we notice that these traits reflect the content of the stereotype formed by the respondents, since they chose multiple traits that have nothing to do with the direct meaning of the term, traits that are neither objective nor accurately depict the individuals who have a neutral position towards the conflict. This stereotype reduces the individuals to the aforementioned traits and categorises them accordingly, irrespective of individual and objective differences among the people who choose to adopt a neutral position in conflicts.

---

[45] Definiton of the term "مندس" (infiltrator) in Almaany dictionary, [online reference], Almaany website: http://goo.gl/MwOCkV, [s.d], reviewed on 07-17-2016.

[46] Bishara, Azmi, *Syria: A Path to Freedom from Suffering*—An Attempt in Contemporary *History, op.cit., p 50–56.*

With regards to the negative impact of the previous stereotypes, some videos that have circulated over social media show members of the security forces and the Syrian army using the stereotype "مُندس" (infiltrator) while torturing and beating opposition members. One video[47] (34th second) shows a person wearing the Syrian military uniform beating and torturing a civilian while calling him "مُندس" (infiltrator), as if the term itself justifies such treatment.

In many videos, the term "شبيح" (thug) is directed as an accusation against the person being punished. For example, one video[48] (53rd second) shows a man in civilian clothing shoot a member of the Syrian security forces from the top of a tall building, shouting "He is a "شبيح" (thug), he is a "شبيح" (thug)".

These examples illustrate the fact that the stereotypes in question have evolved into accusations and proof of guilt against individuals in order to justify the commitment of violent acts against them. The use of these stereotypes thereby justifies the use of violence without resorting to the law or to courts. This clearly demonstrates the negative impact of stereotypes on the societal relations among individuals as well as various communities within Syria.

In light of the results and the analysis conducted on the terms "منحبكجي" (loyalist), "مُندس" (infiltrator), "رمادي" (grey) and "شبيح" (thug), one notices that the previously mentioned theoretical characteristics and elements of stereotypes apply to them all, as stereotypes, just like these terms, reduce the 'other' to certain traits and contain explicit value judgments against them, while lacking objectivity and reliance on personal experience.

The examples mentioned above illustrate the negative impact that these stereotypes have had on social relations among individuals and how they have served as ready-made accusations or traits that justify violence against individuals who have different political views.

---

[47]   Alamat Online, *Torture of a Syrian citizen by the army* (video), [online reference], YouTube, https://goo.gl/8rfSyr, published on 04/07/2012, reviewed on 12/02/2017.

[48]   The Free Syria, "Shabiha" Thrown off Post Office Building in Al Bab, Aleppo (video), [online reference], YouTube, https://goo.gl/G6M35J, published on 14/08/2012, reviewed on 12/02/2017.

Conclusion

In this paper, the researchers have discussed examples of political stereotypes that have emerged during the Syrian uprising, focusing on the emergence of stereotypes and on their routine use and their prominence in Syrian political texts. The paper has also looked into the impact of stereotypes on social relations, noting their clearly negative effects on social relations among individuals and groups in Syrian society.

The paper has also attempted to provide a simple and basic explanation or trajectory of the emergence and use of stereotypes, particularly political stereotypes, by exploring them in the context of the Syrian uprising and the ensuing political texts, using quantitative and qualitative analyses.

The researchers have found, during the course of the study, how stereotypes are formed in political texts by media and political leaders who place the 'others' in a rigid mould that may not necessarily fit them, but rather reduces them to certain traits and issues value judgments against them for particular purposes. These stereotypes also take on a violent dimension, particularly during conflicts and wars. Each party integrates stereotypes into its political texts in order to win over its social or political base and attribute non-objective traits to the 'other', regardless of personal experience with this 'other'. Given the fragility of political discourse in Syria, mainly due to its manipulation by a single political authority for forty years, new terms have emerged during the Syrian uprising, expressing political views that have their own political terminology, and have evolved into stereotypes despite originally expressing individual political positions and views.

The questionnaire conducted as part of the study illustrates the traits of stereotypes formed by some individuals against others, as the results show that these traits have in fact nothing to do with political positions and views, but are rather judgments formed by some individuals against others who have different political views and positions. This has a serious negative impact on the different individuals and groups within society, leading to an increase in violence and perpetuating a culture that consists in abolishing, demonising and stereotyping the different 'other'. By and large, the research undertaken has sought to analyse this phenomenon and to highlight its direct negative impact as a fist step towards addressing it.

In conclusion, it is worth noting that this study does not address the question of how these stereotypes can be broken, but it has attempted to take a first step towards introducing, describing and analysing the concept of 'stereotype' and explaining its connotations and presence in political texts. It is the aim of this study to contribute to any forthcoming research or recommendations on how these stereotypes can be broken or abolished, with the hope of minimising their impact on interaction and relations among individuals and groups within the same society.

Sources and References

Books

Al Badawi, Ahmad Zaki, Glossary of Media Terms, Dar Al Kitab Al Arabi, 1985.

Bishara, Azmi, Syria: A Path to Freedom from Suffering—An Attempt in Contemporary History, Arab Center for Research and Policy Studies, Beirut, 2013.

Marzouk, Asaad, Encyclopedia of Psychology, Arab Institute for Research and Publishing, Beirut, 1987.

Sulayman, Salih, The Media and the Production of Stereotypes, Al Falah Library For Publishing & Distribution, Kuwait, 2005.

English Books

Darity William, *International Encyclopedia of social sciences*, Macmillan Social Science Library, 2008.

Fiske, Susan, and Cuddy, Amy. *Stereotype Content Model*, Journal of Personality and Social Psychology, 2002, VOL.82.

Lippmann. Walter, *Public opinion*, Harcort, Brace Company, 1922.

Moskowitz, Gordon B. *Social Cognition: Understanding Self and Others*, Guilford Press, New York, 2005.

Preston Dyer, *The matter of the images: essays on representations*, London: Routledge, 1993.

Conferences

Iradat Al Jabouri, *Conferences on the Stereotype*, Faculty of Media, University of Baghdad, [s.n], [n.d].

E-dictionaries

Almaany Online: http://www.almaany.com

Dictionary of the Social Sciences – Oxford Reference: www.oxford reference.com

Articles

Al Hajj Salih, Yasin, *On Thugs, Thuggery and their State*, Kalamon magazine, Issue No. 5, Beirut, Winter 2012.

Dabbagh, Basim, *Semiology of the Arabic Suffix "Jee" and its derivatives*, [online reference], Al Modon Online Newspaper, http://tinyurl.com/j4v6dy9, published on 22-03-2014, reviewed on 28-01-2016.

Fairclough, Norman, *Discourse as Social Practice*, translated by Rashad Abd Al Qadir, Al Karmel magazine, Al Karmel Cultural Institution, Issue No. 64, Summer 2000.

Infiltrators exploited the interrogation of crime suspects to launch inciting slogans, [online reference], Al Thawra Newspaper, http://tinyurl.com/j954xgu/, 17-03-2011, reviewed on 14-02-2016.

Infiltrators tour security centers and other institutions claiming they have instructions to police members to use violence, [online reference], Al Thawra Newspaper, http://tinyurl.com/jbb7dbb, 21-03-2011, reviewed on 14-02-2016.

Infiltrators tour security centers and other institutions claiming they have instructions to police members to use violence, [online reference], Al Thawra Newspaper, http://tinyurl.com/jbb7dbb, 9-04-2011, reviewed on 17-02-2016.

Presidential campaign turns into an "oath of allegiance" to Assad in Damascus' streets, [online reference], Al Quds Al Arabi Newspaper, http://www.alquds.co.uk/?p=166848, 12-05-2014, reviewed on 17-02-2016.

The Presidential campaign of Syrian President Bashar Al Assad, [online reference], Asharq Al Awsat, Issue 10407, http://tinyurl.com/h9zsjow, 27-05-2007, reviewed on 09-01-2016.

Shehadeh, Hasib, *Arabic Terms of Turkish Origin*, [online reference], Donia Al Watan Online Newspaper, http://goo.gl/fA5rrp, published on 19-10-2010, reviewed on 7-2-2016.

Shehayid, Jamal, *Anti-regime and Pro-regime Slogans in Syria*, [online reference], Arab Reform Initiative website, http://goo.gl/YXxAea, January 2012, reviewed on 14-07-2016.

The Speech of President Bashar Al Assad to the People's Council, [online reference], Réseau Voltaire website, http://goo.gl/v2exAr, published on 30-03-2011, reviewed on 04-02-2016.

Pictures

Artist Ali Farzat's website: http://www.aliferzat.com/.

Syrian Revolution Stamps, *The Martyr and the Loyalist*, [online reference], The Creative Memory of the Syrian Revolution website, http://goo.gl/tVt8hq, published on 24-02-2013, reviewed on 04-01-2016.

Hani Al Telfah

Born in 1984, Hani Al Telfah studied geography at Damascus University and then continued studies in Mass Communication at the same institution. He worked with the Syrian Trust for Development's project *Massar* within the national programme of tours (the green team). He currently works as a designer of maps with *Mercy Corps* Organisation. He has written many articles for *Ultra Sawt* and the Huffington Post. He has been living in Beirut, Lebanon for three years.

Imagery of the Tormented Body in Contemporary Syrian Art

Prepared by: Mohammad Omran
Supervised by: Marie Elias
Research conducted in 2014–2015

Summary

From the outset of the uprising in Syria, there has been a remarkable presence of Syrian visual artists from different generations keeping abreast of the developments in Syria in their work and indeed contributing to the construction of an imagery that resonates with their country's reality. The tragic events in Syria have left a visible impact on artistic production over the past four years. Despite the divergence of experiences and methods, as well as the striking diversity in representing violence, the tormented human body constitutes the main component in all of these works. Our interest in this topic has thus motivated us to observe and document works that portray the tormented body, which later became the subject of a study entitled *Imagery of the Tormented Body in Contemporary Syrian Art.*

This study is divided into two main axes: the tormented body in Syrian art prior to the revolution, and that which appears in artworks during the revolution. This chronological division aims to measure the differences in the representations of the tormented body in the works of Syrian artists generated by the violent changes from the beginning of 2011 onwards.

The study begins with an introduction that explains the reasons for and the importance of this research and that outlines its methodology. After setting a framework for the analysis, we will provide some background information on the topic of the body in plastic arts in general, as well as the concept of beauty, which differs according to cultures and civilisations. In this section, we will consider how this concept has evolved from ancient times until nowadays. We will then proceed to explain the concept of the tormented body and its meaning in art.

We introduce the first axis by providing an overview of the tormented body in modern Syrian plastic art, briefly showcasing the works of Louay Kayali, Fateh Al Moudarres and Nazir Nabaa, then moving onto Youssef Abdelke and Maher Al Baroudi, before concluding with the experiences of the younger generation, including Yaser Al Safi, Randa Maddah and others.

The first section of this first axis deals with representations of the dead body as one form of the tormented body prior to the revolution.

This, in itself, is divided into two sub-categories: the first deals with the dead body in Syrian art as a symbol of war, as can be seen in the works of Zaki Salam, Mustafa Ali and Assem Al Bacha, whereas the second sub-category deals with the old, contemporary dead body, with Mustafa Ali's *Immortality* as an example. The second section of the axis looks at the notion of the 'monstrous body' in Syrian visual art prior to the revolution, analysing several works by Maher Al Baroudi, Youssef Abdelke, Fadi Yazigi, Sabhan Adam and Randa Maddah. Lastly, the third section tackles the 'sick body' in Syrian art prior to the revolution, with special focus on the works of Maher Al Baroudi, in which psychological illness and insanity are portrayed from the eighties and nineties, stemming from the unique relationship between Al Baroudi and his brother, who suffered from mental health issues.

We then move onto the second axis of our study: namely, how the tormented body is depicted in Syrian visual art during the revolution. We first provide a brief explanation of certain changes that have occurred on the Syrian art scene during this period, by presenting the new subjects and artistic forms that have appeared in the works of some Syrian artists. We then re-divide this axis in a way that loosely corresponds to the structure adopted in the first axis, by exploring the dead body, the fragmented body, the monstrous body and, lastly, the hybrid body.

Following this structure, we first examine the depictions of the dead body in visual art during the revolution. Consequently, this section tackles the dead body as a symbol of the afflicted or ravaged place and reviews and analyses the works of Youssef Baalbaki, Khalil Younes, Akram Al Safadi, Shada Al Safadi and Somar Salam. We then analyse the works of Khalil Younes, Amjad Wardeh, Khaled Al Khani and Dani Abou Louh, which took as a visual reference live-action footage and photographs of violence, such as the case of the child Hamzeh Bakkour. Finally, we address works that have honoured the dead body, under the title of either a known martyr, such as Waseem Marzouki's 'Tribute to Ghiath Matar', or an unknown one, such as Tarek Butayhi's 'The Martyr' or Youssef Abdelke's 'The Martyr's Mother'.

The second section of this axis explores the issue of the fragmented body, which is a ramification of the dead body. It tackles works that depict amputated parts of the human body, especially the decapitated head, such as in the works of Fadi Yazigi, Yaser Al Safi, Omran Younes and Youssef Abdelke. We then move to the monstrous body as depicted in works produced during the revolution, reviewing the works of Azad Hamo, Tarek Butayhi and Akram Al Halabi, before addressing the idea of the 'political monster', as in the works of Monif Ajaj and Hani Charaf. We conclude this axis by exploring the concept of the hybrid body, presenting the works of Khaled Takriti, Fadi Al Hawmi, Sabhan Adam, Kais Selman and Mohannad Orabi.

In the conclusion, we recapitulate the analysis, which mainly revolves around measuring the differences between the representations of the tormented body before and after the revolution.

Introduction

The tormented body in artistic production is considered to be a clear indicator of the level of violence in a given society. In fact, it can be said that the image of the body in any artistic work reflects, in one way or another, that of the society it belongs to. For this reason, we have chosen to track the development of the tormented body in Syrian visual arts, both prior to 2011, which marked the start of the Syrian uprising, and after 2011. By doing so, we may be able to measure some of the changes that have occurred in Syrian society through artistic production.

This research focuses on a selection of artworks from the Syrian repertoire containing images of the tormented body. These images contradict the stereotype of the human body as being beautiful, strong and healthy and constituting a reflection of the human race. We divide the image of the tormented body into different categories, including the 'dead body' in its various forms, such as martyrs, those killed in battlefields or massacres or those who have died naturally. Other categories of the tormented body which we examine include the 'fragmented body', as can be seen in the depiction of amputated limbs for example, and the 'sick body', suffering from a physical or psychological illness. The 'monstrous body' could also be seen as an essential category of the tormented body. 'Monstrous', in this sense, refers to the deformed body, or what is often referred to as the "Grotesque[1]", as well as the hybrid body, inspired from myths and from metaphorical representations of the human body using non-human elements, both animal and mechanical. We can also add to the above the marginalised, oppressed, or frightened body.

---

[1]   "When it first emerged, this term was linked to fine arts, since it was originally attributed to the drawing and decorations discovered in beasts submerged in sand in Italy, with bizarre drawings, such as animals in the shape of vegetables and human faces drawn differently than how they are in reality. Later on, the meaning expanded and the word was used in the science of beauty as an adjective or characteristic given to all that is irregular and bizarre, and all that is funny through exaggeration and deformation, and contrary to exquisite and fine" definition of Grotesque, Marie Elias and Hanane Kassab Hasan, *Al Mu'jam Al Masrahi*, Libairie du Liban Publishers, Beirut, 1997.

Viewing contemporary Syrian artworks from the perspective of their depiction of the tormented body allows us to reconsider the relationship of Syrian society with its new reality. Therefore, the importance of this research lies in the fact that it tackles various aspects that have not been analysed before, at least in terms of the link between the creative product and its historical circumstances. Moreover, following the development of artists who are still active helps us to measure the changes in Syrian society: through the lens of art, we can determine the level of violence permeating every detail of the lives of Syrian people, specifically by examining the appearance of the dead body that has progressed and underwent many transformations over the past few years. It can therefore be viewed as a form of documentation of the widespread death in Syria by alternative means. Furthermore, this research will analyse the artworks that have accompanied and, at times, portrayed the recent developments in Syria. It is thus an attempt to apprehend the relationship between the real image and the imagined one, and to measure the level of violence between the real and the imagined.

The research is divided into two main axes: the tormented body in Syrian visual art (1) prior to and (2) during the revolution. "During the revolution" is perhaps a better way of expressing this period than "after the revolution", since we are still witnessing and living amid the changes that are occurring, and since these experiences are still being accumulated. However, the aim of this chronological division is to measure the differences in the works of Syrian artists caused by the violent changes that started at the outset of 2011, changes that will herein be referred to by the term "revolution"[2].

In this research, we have relied on a chronological sequence of events, whereas in the analysis of the artworks themselves we have opted for a descriptive analysis, considering that every piece of art is, in itself, a text with a real-life reference.

The research presents the works of more than twenty Syrian visual artists of different ages and from various backgrounds and geograph-

---

[2]   Although the term "revolution" might not fully describe what is currently happening, we have adopted it as a main designation in order to facilitate the process of classification and titling, since it is difficult to mention, in every title, additional designations, such as war or crisis, etc.

ical regions. What they have in common, however, is their depiction of the tormented body in their works, both pre- and post-revolution. It is noteworthy to mention that, despite partially being of a documentary nature, this research does not document all the works produced over the past four years, given the difficulty of collecting information under the current situation. For this reason, our main resource in selecting the works was the Internet: our access to artworks was either through the websites of the artists themselves or through other websites that document contemporary Syrian art, such as "The Creative Memory of the Syrian Revolution" and the "Art. Liberty. Syria" Facebook page. At times, we have also had direct communication with artists, be it through Skype, e-mail or, most often, through Facebook.[3]

---

[3]   The names of many Syrian artists from different generations are not mentioned in this research. This is by no means an underestimation of the importance of their work. Specific topics and artists in this research were chosen due to the difficulty in having access to all artistic productions. The selection criteria was largely determined by what artworks were available online, be it prior to or after the revolution, and by the fact that we have mainly focused on what is solely related to the tormented body. Furthermore, in order to document and study all the artworks that are produced during a revolution or war, this revolution or war must come to an end, so that the period of the study can be delimited.

Forward – The Centrality of the Human Body in Art History

Since the dawn of art and until this day, the human body has been the main topic at the center of artistic creation. Portrayals of the human body have evolved and still do, depending on culture, time and place. Moreover, these portrayals can be considered as an indicator of social, economic and political changes occurring in a certain place. In some ancient civilisations, such as the ancient Greek civilisation, the body was a bearer of the idea of perfect beauty, and predominantly represented gods and legendary heroes. This body was therefore "beautiful" and dimensionally harmonious. In one of his major works, "On the Doctrines of Hippocrates and Plato", Galen of Pergamon states that beauty does not lie in the individual elements, but in the harmonious proportion of the parts, in the proportion of one finger in relation to another, of all the fingers to the whole hand, of the rest of the hand to the wrist, of this latter to the forearm, of the forearm to the whole arm."[4]

Venus of Willendorf. Photo: Matthias Kabel via Wikimedia Commons. Licensed under CC BY-SA 3.0 (s. https://creativecommons.org/licenses/by-sa/3.0/deed.en)

---

[4]   Quoted by Eco, Umberto, *Histoire de la beauté*, Paris, Edition Flammarion, 2004, P. 75.

Diego Velasquez, *Venus at Her Mirror* (1650). Source: Wikimedia Commons.
Public Domain.

The law of physical dimensions also differs from one civilisation to another. In fact, ancient Egyptians relied on a net-like grid comprised of even square units that set fixed numeric measurements: the height of the human body must be eighteen units, the length of the foot three units, the length of the arm five units, etc. As for the ancient Greeks, they measure accurate physical dimensions in proportion to the physique: the head is one over eight, while the chest is one over four, etc.

The idea of beauty, specifically the beautiful body, has evolved according to the epoch and civilisation in which it has been produced. For example, the flabby body of Venus of Willendorf, twenty-five thousand years before Christ, looks nothing like Venus's curvy body in Diego Velasquez's painting *Venus at Her Mirror* (1650). It is also worth noting that this naked body could not possibly be further apart from the present-day prevailing concept of the female body, represented by thin models for instance.

Painting by Fernando Botero. Source: Wikimedia Commons.
Public Domain.

In contemporary art, the idea of the body is remarkably diverse: there are as many bodies as artists producing them. Nowadays, we seldom see an artwork that doesn't contain the element of the body in some form, so much so that even highly abstract or conceptual works take it into consideration. As for modernist artists, they build their own vision of the body: cubic for Pablo Picasso, bloated for Fernando Botero, thin for Alberto Giacometti, deformed for Francis Bacon and so on.

The Western contemporary artist has gradually transcended the available means of expression, such as sculpture, painting, photography, engraving and cinematography, going further by using their own body as a main tool to build their artwork, as can be seen in the examples of "Body Art". Orlan (Mireille Suzanne Francette Porte, also known as Orlan), one of the most eminent artists to have adopted this method, says: "I have always perceived my female body, the body of the female artist, as a highly-privileged material in constructing my works (…) my artworks were in a constant quest for the socially-besieged female body."[5]

5   Orlan conférence, *Dans de l'art charnel au baiser de l'artiste*, Paris éditions Jean-Michel Place, 1997, P.34.

Part One – The Tormented Body in Different Art Histories

The tormented body was a central topic in twentieth century Western art, due to the major transformations in Western societies, especially following World Wars I and II. In fact, the impact of these wars on the works of countless Western artists still reflect the violence of that period. Prime examples of this can be seen in Pablo Picasso's painting *Guernica*, and in the war-simulating works of Otto Dix and Ossip Zadkine, alongside many other examples.

However, the extended exploration of the tormented body is not new, as it can be traced back to the ancient Christian representations that portray the body of Christ, the Divine Body, as a bearer of the suffering and pains of the entire world. Several scenes depict the death and torture of Christ: the crucifixion scene by Francisco de Zurbarán (*Saint Luke as a Painter before Christ on the Cross*, 1660), the descent from the cross scene depicted in the work of Rembrandt (*Descent from the Cross*, 1634), the grieving Virgin Mary by Michelangelo (*Pietà*, 1500), the mourning or lamentation scene in Edouard Manet's work (*The Dead Christ with Angels*, 1864), and the burial scene in the work of Hans Holbein the Younger (*The Body of the Dead Christ in the Tomb*, 1521). These examples are indeed representations of the tormented body, but they are far from any notions of deformation due to the concept of beauty adopted at the time.

By a variety of means, western artists have generally stayed true to this heritage that celebrates the notion of the tormented body, despite replacing the "holy" death of Christ with "normal" or "secular" death, and the Great Pains with daily ones. Crucifixion scenes in modern western works acquire a different value that is not necessarily linked in its content to the religious dimension, as seen in the work of Francis Bacon (*Three Studies for a Crucifixion*, 1962).

At the Arab level, this topic has also been related to the violent social and political changes that have occurred, and are still occurring, in the region. In fact, throughout the second half of the twentieth century and until this very day, Arab artists have been producing works that simulate the scenes of blood-shedding in their respective countries.

The most significant of these scenes include the Nakba of 1948, with the establishment of the Zionist project to establish the state of Israel on Palestinian territory; the Naksa of 1967, with the Arab-Israeli war of that year cementing Israeli occupation; the Lebanese civil war and the first and second Gulf wars; and, more recently, the Arab revolutions, most of which have mutated into violent wars. In most of the works of Arab artists depicting the violence unfolding around them, the tormented body stands out as a central element.

First – The Tormented Body in Modern Syrian Art

As argued in this paper, the massive production of the imagery of the tormented body in Syrian visual arts has accompanied the violent events that Syria has witnessed since the outbreak of the revolution in 2011. However, the presence of this imagery in contemporary Syrian art can be traced back to the sixties. This can explain, for instance, artist Louay Kayali's[6] tendency to add an air of melancholia to his characters, as noticed in his work *Then What?* (1965), a painting that reflects the catastrophe inflicted upon the displaced Palestinian people. In fact, he painted *Then What?* two years prior to the Arab-Israeli war, as a kind of premonition, depicting a group of women all wearing black, and two children at either end of the painting, with one of them holding a dove in his hand. We can clearly notice the looks of torment and anguish on their faces, and some have weary, surrendering bodies, while others have their eyes fixated on the sky, for fear of being hit by a shell. The main character in the painting clearly reflects a state of surrender, with their body leaning forward as If about to collapse. Influenced by the 1967 war and the Israeli occupation of the Golan Heights, Fateh Al Moudarres[7], another artist of the same generation, produced a collec-

---

[6]   Louay Kayali (1934–1978) was born in Aleppo. He began studying law at the University of Damascus. After winning a contest organised by the Ministry of Education, he was delegated to Italy to study arts, then came back to Damascus to teach painting in public schools and in the Higher Institute of Fine Arts (later known as the Faculty of Fine Arts). He held several exhibitions in Syria and Italy and died in Aleppo when his room caught fire. There are conflicting stories about the cause of the fire, with some considering it to be an act of suicide, given that the artist suffered from depression.

[7]   Fateh Al Mudarres (1922–1999) was an artist and writer born in Aleppo. He studied at the Accademia di Belli Arte (Academy of Fine Arts) in Rome between 1954 and

tion of works reflecting these events, including *Mothers of Martyrs* (1967). During the sixties, the idea of abstraction prevailed over his work. However, with the beginning of the Arab-Israeli war, he returned to figurative drawing, where all the figures he portrayed were expressive, stylistic, reduced and derived from ancient Orthodox icons. The status of the bodies in the painting is similar to that of Kayali's, where a group of persons of different sizes are standing, suggesting they are of different ages, with an obvious sense of panic on their faces, reflected by the motionless postures of their bodies.

Louay Kayali, *Then What* (1965). Reprinted with kind permission.

Artist Nazir Nabaa[8] also embodied the calamity of the 1967 war through his painting *Napalm* (1967), the name of which was inspired

---

1960, and at the Ecole des Beaux Arts, Paris, for three years during the early seventies. He then returned to Damascus to teach at the Faculty of Fine Arts. He has participated in several local and international exhibitions and headed the Syndicate of Fine Arts for a long period of time.

[8]   Nazir Nabaa was born in 1938 in Damascus. He graduated from the Photography Department at the Faculty of Fine Arts in Cairo, Egypt in 1965, and pursued his training at the École Nationale Supérieure des Beaux-Arts, Paris, in 1972. He studied for a long time at the Faculty of Fine Arts and worked in journalism, illustrations and children's books drawings. In addition to his writings on visual arts, he held several

from the napalm firebombs used during the Vietnam War. The portrayed figure is in a state of sheer terror, with bulging eyes, a wide-open shouting mouth and a contracted body, all reflecting the enormity of the tragedy.

Despite their difference in technique or style, what the three aforementioned works have in common is the topic of the tormented body, incarnated in three frightened figures awaiting death.

The Lebanese civil war[9] had an impact on Syrian art as well, as can be seen in Naim Ismail's[10] *Postcard* (1975), depicting three armed men in different colours, referencing their sectarian affiliations, preceded by a dead woman's body, symbolising Beirut.

Sculptor Zuhair Dabbagh (1953–) based his graduation project on the 1976 Tel Al Zaatar massacre[11]; but all works at the time were destroyed by Intelligence Forces. Sculptor Rabih Al Akhras (1951–) also had a project on the same topic.

Youssef Abdelke, *September Trilogy* (1976). Reprinted with kind permission.

The tormented body is also present in Youssef Abdelke's triptych, *September Trilogy* (1976), which was his graduation project for the Faculty

---

solo and group exhibitions in various cities. He was awarded the Syrian Order of Civil Merit, Excellent Class.

[9]   The Lebanese civil war erupted in April 1975 and ended in October 1990. The conflict, which cost 150,000 lives, injured 300,000 and led to the emigration of almost a million people, brought the Lebanese state to near collapse.

[10]   Visual artist Naim Ismail (1930–1979) was born in the northern city of Antioch. He graduated from the Faculty of Fine Arts, Istanbul in 1953 and worked as an artistic supervisor in Jaysh Al Sha'ab magazine from 1958 until 1970, and as a director of fine arts between 1970 and 1979.

[11]   Tel Al Zaatar (the Hill of Thyme) was a Palestinian refugee camp established in 1948 in the northern part of what later became Christian East Beirut during the Lebanese civil war of 1975–1990. As part of the internal political power games at the beginning of the war, Tel-el-Zaatar was besieged and a substantial part of its population was massacred.

of Arts in Damascus. In the central painting, we can see a military general depicted as a monster standing in the middle, with tanks and artilleries protruding from behind him, marching over the bodies of horses and men. In the side paintings, men, women and children are in a state of protest and resistance.

Maher Al Baroudi, *Salute to the Leaders* (1979). Reprinted with kind permission.

In the wall sculpture, *Salute to the Leaders* (1979), which was a part of sculptor Maher Al Baroudi's graduation project in 1979, also inspired by the Tel Al Zaatar massacre, we can see men with sinister features, mockingly laughing at human body parts laid in front of them. These grotesque shapes bring to mind the sculptures of French artist Honoré Daumier in his work *The Celebrities of the Juste Milieu* (1932/1935), although the latter is closer to caricature in its style. In addition to this work, Al Baroudi also produced a collection addressing the topic of famine, where he used the emaciated body of the child to depict the humanitarian disasters hitting parts of Africa at the time.

In examining the aforementioned works, one can clearly notice that the common factor amongst them is the element of the tormented body. Using this element might be an axiomatic step, since it is perhaps the clearest and most straightforward tool for commenting on an ongoing event. It is therefore difficult to find, in general, a work of

124

art tackling a violent event such as a massacre without depicting a dead body. In this case, using the body can be seen as more of a message of objection to death and violence.

Despite the bloody events that took place in the eighties, such as the Hama massacre in Syria in 1982[12] and the Sabra and Shatila massacre[13] in Lebanon in the same year, no works pertaining to these two events were seen in the artistic repertoire, not publicly at least. However other Arab artists, such as Kuwaiti sculptor Sami Mohammed and Iraqi artist Dia Azzawi, resorted to the tormented body as a means to express the atrocity of the crimes perpetrated by the Lebanese right-wing forces, in collaboration with the Israeli occupation forces, in the Sabra and Shatila camps.

The Hama massacre might be the most problematic issue, as the secrecy around the matter transformed it into a taboo in Syrian society under the Baath regime. In addition to that, the scarcity of photographs documenting the massacre made the incident a topic that is hard to represent. As a result, it was not until 2011, more than 29 years after the massacre, a representation of the massacre appeared in visual arts, particularly in *Hama 30*(2012) by artist Khalil Younes (1980–).

Indeed, the main feature in the expression of violence is centered around the element of the dead body, something that will make its comeback with the outset of the 2011 revolution in Syria. In contrast, some other forms of the tormented body might not be represented as often, such as the sick, exhausted and marginalised body, depicted particularly in the works of Maher Al Baroudi, who has dealt with this issue as a result of his brother's mental illness.

---

[12] "The **Hama massacre** occurred on 2 February 1982, when the Syrian Arab Army and the Defense Companies, under the orders of the country's president Hafez Al Assad, besieged the town of Hama for 27 days in order to quell an uprising by the Muslim Brotherhood against Al Assad's government. (...) The attack has been described as one of the single deadliest acts by any Arab government against its own people in the modern Middle East." https://en.wikipedia.org/w/index.php?title =1982_Hama_massacre&oldid=814981868

[13] The Sabra and Shatila massacre occurred on September 16, 1982, following the Israeli invasion of Lebanon, when the right-wing Christian Phalange militia stormed the Sabra and Shatila refugee camps in West Beirut and began a massacre which ended in the deaths of hundreds, maybe thousands, of mostly Palestinian civilians. For more info see https://en.wikipedia.org/wiki/Sabra_and_Shatila_massacre

Other images of the tormented body, such as the (deformed) monstrous or 'grotesque' body, can be found in "satirical" representations of the dictator. This can be seen, for example, in the 'People' collection by Youssef Abdelke[14] (monster-like men in power) from the early nineties, and in the portraits of Maher Al Baroudi[15] (monster-like generals) produced around the same time period. The melancholic body was depicted in the works of Safwan Dahoul (1961-) in the late nineties (broken bodies, dead black eyes). Moreover, there is a clear predilection for the deformed body, which is close to the concept of the monster, in the works of Sabhan Adam (1973-) and Fadi Yazigi (1966–) who brings together animal and human bodies (the 'hybrid' body). Both experiences emerged during the late nineties, on the cusp of the millennium. This can also be seen in the works of Yaser Al Safi (1976–), where the deformed body resembles a childish expressive status, or those of Omran Younes (1971), where the body is in a state of convulsion. This contradicts the works of Kais Selman (1976), who, like Austrian artist Egon Schiele for example, perceives the notion of ugliness as a synonym for beauty, rather than an opposite thereof. Mention should be also made of the works of Iman Hasbani (1979–) who has repeatedly depicted monsters in her portraits.

The frightened body can be seen in the works of Nisrine Boukhari (1981–), Randa Maddah (1983–) and Yamen Yousef (1982–), where the body appears fat and lacks a clear gender identity. Numerous examples can be given, noting that the tormented body is represented in

---

[14] Youssef Abdelke was born in Qamishli in 1951. He graduated from the Engraving Department atthe Faculty of Fine Arts in 1976, and obtained his diploma from the École Nationale Supérieure des Beaux-Arts, Paris, in 1986, and his PhD from Université Paris 8 in 1989. He became known for his caricatures and children drawings, as well as his poster designs. During the late seventies, he was arrested for two years for his political activity and left for Paris after his release. He came back to Damascus in 2005 to found his own atelier. He currently lives in Damascus.

[15] Maher Al Baroudi was born in Damascus in 1955. He graduated from the Sculpture Department in the Université de Lyon in 1979, pursued his education in France and obtained his first diploma from the École Nationale Supérieure des Beaux-Arts de Lyon, in 1982, and his second one from the École Nationale Supérieure des Beaux-Arts, Paris, in 1983. He worked as an assistant in Damascus University in 1980 and 1981 and was a sculpture and drawing professor at the School of Applied Arts, Lyon in 1985–1986. Since 1996, he has been a professor in Emile Cohl School in Lyon, France, where he currently lives.

different ways and forms in the works of most Syrian artists, from modernists to contemporaries. This general tendency towards the form of the tormented body gained momentum at the beginning of the third millennium, and it could be attributed to the desire to discover new potentials for the body, outside the framework of the academic concept, not to mention the growing state of pressure and despair, especially among the youth, which might have helped in consolidating this tendency.

Second – The Dead Body in Syrian Arts Prior to the Revolution

Death is undeniably one of the most discussed themes in the history of art, not only because it is a formative part of the human psyche and the inevitable fate of all humans, but also because it is tightly linked to all the core values of human civilisation. Man dies, yet his memory lingers, perpetuated by art. This might be the explanation behind the baffling number of scenes and images that celebrate death daily. In this regard, Michel Onfray[16] says:

> Sex, blood and death intrinsically nurture and nourish the history of art. How abundant are the scenes of war, crimes, crucifixion, slaughter, rape, suicide, hanging and torture. How exuberant is the shed blood and how many are the decapitated heads, hung on the museums walls, from the walls of the Lascaux, through the works adorned by the stories of Christian martyrs, to the classic paintings of war. They are the lightning disturbing the serenity of summer nights, leaving under the star-studded sky ephemeral, albeit burning traces.[17]

In its presentation of death, modern western art has relied explicitly on religious references. However, this death has become similar to other forms of art, which means that it is no longer as sacred as it once was. The death of Christ has now become similar to that of a civilian on the street or a militant at war, or even to that of an ill person on his death-bed.

---

[16]   Michel Onfray is one of the most prominent contemporary philosophers in France. In 2002, he founded, along with his friends, the "Popular University" under the slogan "philosophy for all".

[17]   Onfray Michel, *Catalogue Vladimir Velickovic – Blessure(s)*, Fondation Coprim, *Paris, 2002*, p 7.

War, as a source of psychological and visual violence, was and still is the most influential subject for the twentieth century artist and the greatest trigger of his imagination. How could it not be such when this century has brought some of the most abominable wars in the history of mankind!

Third – The Dead Body in Syrian Art as a Symbol of War

In general, most of pre-revolution Syrian works depicting the dead body were either linked to the idea of war or symbolised a place or homeland destroyed by humans. Palestine in particular became a central motivation for the creativity of Syrian and Arab artists, who produced their works as an expression of solidarity with the cause of the Palestinian people.

Zaki Salam, *The Martyr* (2005). Reprinted with kind permission.

In a sculpture by Syrian-Palestinian artist Zaki Salam[18] entitled *The Martyr* (2005), the martyr's body is bigger than those of his mourners. The martyr has one hand open towards the sky, as if wanting to communicate with it, while despair and pain can be seen on the mourners' faces. Some faces are looking at the sky; a child, recognised as such by being smaller than others, is crying, with his hand on the goat that

---

[18]   Syrian Palestinian sculptor Zaki Salam was born in 1958 in Damascus. In 1984, he graduated from the Sculpture Department of the Faculty of Fine Arts, Damascus, and headed the Porcelain Department of the Institute of Applied Arts, Damascus, from 1984 until 2008. He also participated in several solo and group exhibitions in Syria, Jordan, Bahrain, Spain and Italy. He currently lives in Algeria.

joins the crowd. Here we are, before a lamentation scene, amidst a funeral where parents, relatives and friends are gathered to carry a dead body as big as their tragedy. In this work, the body is Palestine.

In Mustafa Ali's[19] *A Woman from Gaza* (2009), the dead body of a woman, curled in the foetal position, is placed against a square bronze slab. It calls to mind the preserved corpses that resulted from the 79 AD volcanic explosion of Mount Vesuvius in Pompeii. The artist uses slivers of wood to suggest the debris of an attack, but breaks this status of death by adding an electrical device that restores the heartbeat, as an act of resistance.

Assem Al Bacha, *Embryo* (2002). Reprinted with kind permission.

In his wall sculpture *Embryo* (2002), Assem Al Bacha[20] depicts several hands, sculpted out of plaster from a real-life mould, arranged together in a tight space. Positioning the hands as such makes them look as if they are floating on water, or, to the contrary, diving into a pool of

---

[19]   Sculptor Mustafa Ali was born in Latakia in 1956. In 1979, he graduated from the Faculty of Fine Arts, Damascus, and continued his studies at the Accademia di Belle Arti di Carrara (Academy of Fine Arts), Carrara, Italy, graduating in 1996. He is the founder and owner of a cultural institution and an art gallery bearing his name in Old Damascus. He currently lives in Damascus.

[20]   Sculptor and writer Assem Al Bacha was born in 1948 in Buenos Aires, Argentina. In 1957, he moved with his family to Syria and studied Philosophy at Damascus University in 1968. He then studied sculpture at the Faculty of Fine Arts and obtained his Master's degree in Monumental Sculpture from Moscow University. Among his novels: Wa-ba'd min ayyam ukhar (And Something from Other Days), 1984. He has been living in Granada, Spain, since 1987.

mud. The fists seen in the sculpture are reminiscent of the human remains found under the debris of shelled houses. This work was an act
of solidarity with the Palestinians in a refugee camp in the West Bank
which was shelled by Israeli forces in 2002.

Forth – Old, Contemporary Dead Body

Not only contemporary instances of violence have inspired the depiction of dead bodies in the works of Syrian artists. Many have also
drawn inspiration from the myths and ancient civilisations of the region, replicating old motifs and subjects from a contemporary angle.
Again, this can be seen in the works of sculptor Mustafa Ali who
touched on death and immortality in his sculpture *Mummy or Immortality* (1995).

In this work, we see a motionless body lying in a glass cube elevated on four bronze pillars, with the head of a jackal placed on the glass
cube, the tomb. This sculpture reminds us of the arte facts seen in archaeological museums. Here, the influence of ancient civilisations on
the artist could not be clearer, as the image of the dead body immediately recalls the Egyptian mummy, explicitly expressed in the title of
the work. In addition to that, the jackal's head embodies the Egyptian
God Anubis worshipped by Ancient Egyptians.

Fifth – The Monstrous Body in Syrian Art
Prior to the Revolution

Maher Al Baroudi, *The Activist*. Reprinted with kind permission.

Maher Al Baroudi, *The Tie*   Maher Al Baroudi, *Forever*
Reprinted with kind permission

According to a description by Sally O'Reilly, "the term monster is usually used to refer to what goes beyond the human logic or to the things that do not fall under the general model or the specific criteria set by men"[21].

---

[21]   O'Reilly Sally, *Le corps dans l'art contemporain*, Edition Thames et Hudson, Paris, 2010, P. 149

Between 1990 and 1991, Maher Al Baroudi produced four portraits, including the diptych *The Activist*, in addition to *The Tie* and *Forever*. All four paintings showcase monstrous creatures wearing military uniforms covered in fake medals, fashioned out of soft drink bottle caps.

The artist herein incorporates in his works a clear and direct political discourse. He is mocking the image of the dictator, turning him into a clownish monster who is wearing fake medals of victory. It is worth noting that the artist had previously used fake medals in other works, such as *The Game* (1986), inspired by an ill person incarnating a general, someone that Al Baroudi used to see during his visits to his brother in the Douma psychiatric hospital. He says: "Real insanity is indeed what we see in psychiatric hospitals. Nevertheless, there are other types of insanity, such as the man in power who would do everything to maintain his power".[22]

Youssef Abdelke's capacity to alter shapes is unequivocally reflected in his work, particularly in his collection entitled *People* (1989–1995).The collection, which he started in the late eighties and continued until the mid-nineties, consists of a number of engravings and works executed in various techniques such as pastel.

---

[22]   Mohammad Omran, *Interview with Maher Al Baroudi*, [s.l.], 2008, [s.n]

Youssef Abdelke, *People* (1989–1995). Reprinted with kind permission.

Despite their different techniques, what all these works have in common is the act of delving into the meaning of ugliness and violence. In this picture he mockingly and violently draws the image of the dictator, likening him to a monster. The central figure is gazing through a glass eye, an element probably added by collage; with a mouth wide open showing its animal teeth. The official uniform and the medal clearly indicate a man in power. Similar to other paintings of the same collection, one can clearly notice the alterations of the head; it is sometimes surrounded by an aureole. At other times the number of medals grows, further mocking the man in power, or the dictator. At the right side of the painting, another figure appears with almost the same features, but smaller in size. It is the "monster" standing on what looks like a hanger, with its arm on its master's shoulder for protection. On the left is a female body with a banana for a head, at the bottom of which there are several shoes and an amputated leg. In this work, as in many others, Abdelke is inspired by the idea of a trinity, which appears to be a symbol of military power: money, religion and sex. It also ridicules the idea of the trinity that was sanctified in Syria through the image of former president Hafez Al Assad and his two sons as symbols of Syrian sovereignty. Even the vivid colours the artist opted for cannot alleviate the violence inherent in this painting. Additionally, the disassembled body parts, like the hands, and their re-instalment in places other than their natural position, contributes to increasing the level of violence of the entire piece.

Sabhan Adam[23] is yet another Syrian artist who has worked extensively on the topic of the monstrous body. His works stood out during the late nineties, on the brink of the third millennium. The ugliness of the creatures that Adam draws is shocking: faces with bulging, sometimes duplicated eyes looking in all directions, thin bodies wearing coloured clothes. At other times the bodies are hybrid, combining a human head and an animal body, as seen in his painting *Bird Man*, where he placed a human head on a bird's body, reminding us of the Greek mythological figure Harpies.[24] In fact, beauty, in its conventional concept, is often not what triggers an artist's creativity; it is rather the ugliness represented in these gruesome faces. According to the poet

---

[23] A self-made artist born in 1973, in Al Hasakah. He is one of the most internationally well-known Syrian artists. He organised several solo exhibitions all around the world, the last of which was in Polad-Hardouin Gallery, Paris.

[24] Mythical creatures of the Greek civilisation, responsible for disappearances, epidemics and famines. From Martial Guédron's book, *Monsters, marvels and fantastic creatures (Monstres, merveilles et créatures fantastiques)*, Hazan, Paris, 2011, p. 75

Adonis, ugliness uncovers the crisis of human expression, revealing all that manages to escape the restrictions of the mind. He says: "They are creatures living in my head. They might have human features or could possibly be an animal combination. But at the end of the day, they are my creation and they do not have a healing answer to questions about their origin and the stages of their becoming".[25]

Fadi Yazigi, *King Quasimodo* (2008). Reprinted with kind permission.

The world of Fadi Yazigi[26] may seem far from the topic of the torment-ed body, as an overview of his artistic output prior to the revolution reveals the presence of smiling childish creatures and other beings such as petbirds and donkeys, etc. Nevertheless, there is a kind of hidden cruelty in these works, a cruelty that appears in the dwarfing pro-portions that he chose for his characters, so as to give the impression that they are being confined and pressured, although floating in the space of the painting sometimes. In some instances, Fadi Yazigi resorts to a combination of the human and the animal body, as in his *King*

---

[25]   *Nawal Al Ali, Interview with Adonis,* Al Akhbar Lebanese newspaper, issue number 268, 2007.

[26]   Sculptor and painter born in Latakia in 1966. He graduated from the Sculpture Department of the Faculty of Fine Arts, Damascus, in 1988. He has had several solo and group exhibitions in various countries. He currently resides in Damascus.

Quasimodo (2008), where the body looks more like that of a little puppy, while the head is that of a human. This title of the work refers to the character of Quasimodo in Victor Hugo's novel *The Hunchback of Notre Dame*, possibly because it embodies the idea of the benevolent monster. As for the hybrid body in this sculpture, it resembles the Sphinx.

This tendency to "deform" or play with anatomic proportions, suggesting new atypical patterns for body parts and exaggerating proportions, is generally becoming a common feature in many works by the newer generation of artists. The works of Yaser Al Safi, Kais Selman, Iman Hasbani, Yamen Yousef, Nisrine Boukhari, Alaa Abu Shaheen and others are great examples for this trend.

The work of Randa Maddah[27] from the occupied Golan might be the most flagrant one to express the notion of the monstrous body, especially in her installation *Without Annunciations* (2010), which was exhibited in Jerusalem as a part of the 'On the Gates of Heaven' festival in 2010.

In this installation, Maddah's tormented creatures are distributed in a confined white rectangular chamber. In the front, the work shows a head with a long neck coming out of the wall, with two hands wrapped around it. In the back there is a body with two human heads, a hermaphrodite[28], with its arms pinned to the back and its legs stretched to the front. Another creature hangs from a chair dangled from the ceiling. On the opposite wall a decapitated head, whose long neck is being strangled by two hands, protrudes from the wall. Underneath it, on the floor, the remains of two dead bodies can be seen. A diabolical scene indeed! The creatures and monsters in this work call to mind the disturbing imaginary worlds of Dutch painter Hieronymus Bosch. The grotesque creatures in this and other works by Randa Mad-

---

[27] Randa Maddah was born in Majdal Shams in 1983. She graduated from the Sculpture Department of the Faculty of Fine Arts in Damascus in 2005. She is a founding member of Fateh Al Moudarres Center for Arts and Culture in the occupied Syrian Golan. She has participated in several group exhibitions and sculpture symposiums, and directed in 2014 a short film entitled "Light Horizon" that was featured in several film festivals.

[28] "A body that combines the body of a man and that of a woman at the same time, expressing the idea of perfection at times, or that of disdain and vulgarity at others." From Martial Guédron's book, *Monsters, marvels and fantastic creatures (Monstres, merveilles et créatures fantastiques)*, Hazan, Paris, 2011, p. 111.

136

dah, once again raise questions about the intricate historical relationship between the artist and the monster, as well as the symbolic dimensions attributed by the artist to the horrifying figures.

Randa Maddah, *Without Annunciations* (2010). Reprinted with kind permission.

Sixth – The Sick Body in Syrian Art
Prior to the Revolution

Works using "the sick body" as a main feature are not abundant in the Syrian art repertoire, especially those tackling physical illness. Amongst the younger generation, some do employ this element, as can be seen in sculptor Maysan Salman's (1984–) statue of a naked man's body, wobbling with one hand on his head and the other on his stomach as if he was injured and dying. Another work by sculptor Alaa Abou Shaheen (1983–) depicts the body of a one-legged woman leaning on a cane.

As for psychological illness or insanity, this is mainly portrayed in the works of Maher Al Baroudi. His unique relationship with his schizophrenic brother is one of the most important issues embodied in his artwork. Al Baroudi used to visit his brother at a psychiatric hospital in Douma while still a student at the Faculty of Arts in Damascus. His brother's condition was the motive behind his increased interest in the topic of psychological illness, and during his visits, he managed to conduct some studies on patients there. In this regard, Al Baroudi says: "The sanatorium is like a prison; some patients were locked in cells as if they were dangerous criminals".[29]

In addition to the topic of insanity, Al Baroudi was also interested in alcoholic homeless persons he encountered in train stations and fringe areas in Lyon, France, where he lives. The sick body thus became Al Baroudi's main topic during the eighties and nineties; it embodies the idea of the marginalised man, victim of violence and social rejection.

---

[29]   Mohammad Omran, *Interview with Maher Al Baroudi*, op. cit.

Maher Al Baroudi, *Between Us* (1982). Reprinted with kind permission.

One of Al Baroudi's first works on the subject of insanity is a painting entitled *Between Us* (1982) where he portrays a group of people who, at first glance, appear to be different characters due to their different clothes and postures. However, it turns out that they are all one character in various positions and situations: one man sitting on the bench in the front of the painting, another one in the center of the painting, a person raising his hands imitating a bird, behind him a person smoking a cigarette, and one in the back with a dove on his head. In reality they are all multiple possibilities for a single character. As for the space the artist has chosen for his figures, it evokes the impression of deserted places, with a door resembling the entrance of a cave. The doves in the back elicit a feeling of cold, as if this character, in his various possibilities, has left or moved from one world to another through this gate.

Maher Al Baroudi, *With the Passing of Time* (1989). Reprinted with kind permission.

In another work, *With the Passing of Time* (1989), we see two seemingly homeless men sleeping peacefully, wearing dark blue clothes. In front of them, a man wearing a tattered coat tries desperately to remove a mask stuck to his face. This character represents Al Baroudi's brother when his condition worsens. The artist painted his brother in his different states, as if recording the stages of his psychological disorder.

Part Two – The Tormented Body in Artworks Produced during the Syrian Revolution

Ever since the beginning of the uprising in Syria in March 2011, one could notice a strong presence of visual artists from different generations interacting with the developments in Syria and contributing to the making of its image. This has already led to the production of a conspicuous impact of artworks over the past four years. In fact, most artworks were conceived with the intention of causing a shock similar to that engendered by the daily violence ravaging the country. The tragic developments in Syria may have led to transformations in the artist's relationship with the Syrian cause, as reflected in his or her relationship with their tools and creative production.

Through the use of social media, most artists were capable of expressing their stance on what is happening in the country. Despite the various subjects and different styles employed by each of them, the element of the tormented body, as well as the images of war and destruction, have undeniably had the strongest presence in all artistic productions. This certainly chimes with other art repertoires in different countries that have undergone similar circumstances, as seen for instance in the Lebanese and Iraqi experiences over the past few decades.

Some of these artists have had a drastic shift from what they had produced before the revolution. Artist Youssef Abdelke, who for a long time had taken still life as a main topic in his work, veered towards figurative art. His first painting simulating the Syrian ordeal was *A Martyr from Daraa 1* (2011).

Works by artist Abdul Karim Majdal Al Beik (1973–), whose attention in the past was mainly focused on observing time go by and drawing its traces on walls, such as the traces of rain, children's scribbles, teenagers' writings and obituaries, later on became dominated by subjects expressing death and war, such as crosses, knives, traps, diverse weapons and bullets. The tormented body is also manifested in the works of Omran Younes (1971–). This theme and its sub-divisions were not absent from his works prior to the revolution. However, in time, their presence grew stronger, especially over the past two years, during which Younes has produced a black and white collection, using only pencil and charcoal, and another coloured collection with inks and aqua colour, entitled *Miniatures of Syrian Death (2014)*, where the dead body is a central theme.

Prior to the revolution, the topics tackled by photographer Jaber Al Azmeh (1973–) were diversified, before moving towards a symbolic documentation of violence and death, as in his *Wounds* collection, where he shot shadows of persons in a sea of red as the colour of death.

In contrast, some artists have largely maintained their direction of work as it has been in the pre-revolution period, but we can see that the element of the tormented body has gained more presence. This is for example noticeable in the recent works of Safwan Dahoul (1961–), such as *Dream* (2014), where the element of the dead body appears in colours that seem darker than those he used to work with before.

Edward Shahda, *Syria* (2011). Reprinted with kind permission.

In his work, Edward Shahda (1952–) revisits some previously-tackled subjects, among which we can find the subject of the dead body. In his painting *Syria* (2011) for example, the crucified Christ symbolises the contemporary Syrian human being. In the latest works of sculptor Assem Al Bacha, the dead body emerges remarkably as a topic, mainly in his copper oxide ceramics, such as *A Syrian Scene*, where a father is carrying his deceased son, or *The Road to Baba Amr*, where we see indistinct figures elevated on crosses.

Reem Yassouf's works (1979–) are also closely connected to her previous experience, but the presence of the child's body as a main element in her post-revolution paintings is highly noticeable, as a sort of tribute to the souls of children who lost their lives during the war. This can be seen for example in one element of Yassouf's latest collection, *Cold Breezes*, where, in the center of the painting, she portrays the bent body of a little girl raising her arms, indicating a state of flight– or perhaps death– with a flock of swallows accompanying her on her journey.

First – New Artistic Subjects and Shapes

Some artists have changed or diversified the media they use, as is the case in the works of Khalil Younes (1980–), who produced, during the early period of the revolution, a series of drawings entitled *Revolution,* which are characterised by special harshness and blatancy. Most of these works relied on real images as a visual reference.

In 2012, Shada Al Safadi (1982–) presented an installation entitled *Promises,* simulating the idea of a massacre. The artist engraved body traces on Plexiglas, while the lighting shed on these traces drew their ghost-like shadows on the gallery's walls. Speaking about this work, Al Safadi says: "This soul could have soared without being seen, but the enormity of the massacre, as well as the wallow of the soul in fear, led it to leave a trace".[30]

Akram Al Halabi (1981–) focused mainly on reproducing images and adding defining words to them, such as in his photomontage collection, where he reproduced images of the massacres perpetrated in Syria, thus showcasing his visual definition of violence. In addition to the tormented body, new subjects emerged in the Syrian art repertoire, including "the mortar", as seen in a painting by Mohannad Orabi

---

[30]   Mohammad Omran, *Interview with Shada Al Safadi*, [s.l.], 2012, [s.n]

(1977–) where at the first level, a mortar shell is placed before a face surrounded by a red halo, becoming an integral part of his identity.

Another example is *Light Horizon,* a film by Randa Maddah, in which she herself is featured tidying up a room of a house destroyed by the 1967 Israeli aggression on Ain Fit village, the artist's hometown located in the occupied Golan. When she finishes cleaning, she clears the place and puts a white projectile on the table. Although the film needs no additional detail, putting the projectile in this context gives it a quotidian character and makes it an ordinary item.

In a work by Yaser Al Safi (1976–), a man is portrayed at the center of the painting holding a pistol and threatening the other "creatures" floating in the work space. Amidst the context of the current developments in Syria, it is indeed hard to consider the element of the pistol in Al Safi's painting as a mere ordinary figurative subject. "The pistol" is also present in the works of Abdul Karim Majdal Al Beik, as for example in a painting entitled *The Night* (2012), where several pistols are scattered on a square black patch. All this use of weapons as a main element in the structure of the painting only indicates the increasing violence in Syrian society.

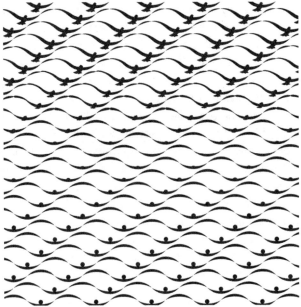

Dino Ahmad Ali, *Across the Sea* (2013). Reprinted with kind permission.

It is worth noting that topics such as migration and refugees have begun to emerge in artworks, especially over the past two years, as in *Migration Across the Sea* (2013) by Dino Ahmad Ali (1985–), who works mainly on posters creating optical illusions. We can see the simplified repeated and intertwined shape of a drowning man's head turning progressively into a bird.

Second – The Dead Body, Symbol of the Afflicted Country

Youssef Abdelke, *A Martyr from Daraa*, (2011). Reprinted with kind permission.

The theme of the dead body has clearly surfaced in the post-revolution productions of most artists. Some of the titles include names of cities and towns that were violently oppressed by the Syrian regime, thus turning the dead body into a symbol of the afflicted place.

In Youssef Abdelke's *A Martyr from Daraa*, (2011), a man is seen lying on a sidewalk, with his hand trying to suppress the flow of blood caused by a bullet that penetrated his body. His pale face indicates his approaching death, while his eyes are scared and shocked, not expecting his death. His mouth is slightly open as if wanting to tell us something. The body lies in the lower part of the work and intersects with the sidewalk line. The painting looks unfinished, for the artist only emphasised the face and the hands, leaving the other parts undone. This evokes portraits produced post-mortem to immortalise the memory of the deceased.

In *Hama 30* (2012), Khalil Younes[31] depicts a nude female torso against a black background. The title of the work commemorates the 30th anniversary of the Hama massacre. The blood, represented by the red colour, prevails over the torso, except for the breast area where we see marks of stitches left from the removal of the nipples. The intended bluntness of the image raises, once again, questions about a topic perceived as taboo before the revolution; a wound in the Syrian collective memory that has yet to heal.

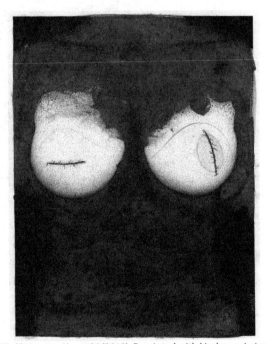

Khalil Younes, *Hama 30* (2012). Reprinted with kind permission.

[31]   Khalil Younes is a painter, visual artist and writer. He was born in Damascus in 1983 and moved to the USA in 1998 to study Cinematography at Columbia College of Chicago. He obtained a degree in experimental film and video from the Massachusetts College of Art and Design of Boston. He currently lives in Chicago.

In Akram Al Halabi's *A Syrian Boy or Karm Al Zaytoun*(2012), we see four indistinct children's bodies with English words like hand, eye, face, arm, leg and child, all scattered on top of them, as if the artist is seeking to redefine these dead bodies by naming their parts. This image, executed through Photoshop and taken from a video that was posted online after the 2012 Karm Al Zaytoun massacre, is part of Al Halabi's visual collection addressing the revolution, where the artist suggests a new rapport between image and writing, as well as between death and art.

Another work entitled *Karm Al Zaytoun* (2012) by Shada Al Safadi[32] shows a reclining body with six hands wrapped around it, in addition to its own, as if someone were pulling it to the back. At the center, next to the body, is a sad-looking child carrying under his arm what looks like an unspecified book, with a small black cloud next to him pouring black rain.

Shada Al Safadi, *Karm Al Zaytoun* (2012). Reprinted with kind permission.

---

[32] Born in Majdal Shams (the occupied Golan) in 1982, Shada Al Safadi studied engraving at Adham Ismail Center in Damascus in 2004 and graduated from the Photography Department at Damascus University in 2006. She has participated in several exhibitions and obtained a three-month artist residency in the city of arts, Paris, in 2004.

147

In the drawing *From Houla to the Sky* (2012) by artist Somar Sallam[33], we see dead bodies against an impure orange background, ascending to the sky in an upside down position, thus challenging the stereotypical depiction of souls ascending to the sky. Despite their different ages and appearances–some of them are chained with ropes, simulating the true image of the massacre– all the bodies share the same features, as if belonging to the same family.

In contrast to the previously mentioned works, the woman in Saoud Al Abdallah's[34] painting might not be dead, despite being portrayed in a similar posture. We can see a woman's body covered by a black cloak, under which we can see a miniature face and feet that look contracted. The woman, identified in the title as *A Woman from Douma* (2014), is leaning on a wall that can be differentiated from the floor by a separating line dividing the painting into two equal parts.

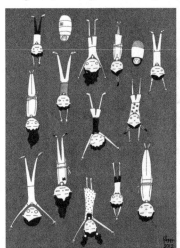

Somar Sallam, *From Houla to the Sky* (2012) Saoud Al Abdallah, *A Woman from Douma* (2014)
Reprinted with kind permission

[33]   Coming from a Palestinian family, Somar Sallam was born in 1988 in Damascus. She graduated from the Photography Department at Damascus University in 2012. She works as a children's illustrator in various publishing houses. She has participated in several exhibitions in Damascus, Homs and Algeria where she currently lives, after recently moving there with her family.

[34]   Saoud Al Abdullah was born in Al Hasakah in 1976. He obtained a BA from the Oil Painting Department at the Faculty of Fine Arts, Damascus in 2005 and a Master's degree in the same major in 2007. He has participated in several exhibitions, the last of which was in Art on 56th Gallery, Beirut in 2014. He currently lives in Beirut.

In addition to the works that document afflicted cities through the body, other works reproducing the image of real death have emerged as well, with the dead or fragmented body as their main element. As with many others, these works were mostly based on real images of violence and on graphic videos posted online. It seems that the intensity of daily real-life violent scenes have pushed artists to choose whatever they find 'attractive' in them.

Such 'attraction' might arise from the shock generated by the cruelty of the image, as in the incident of Hamzeh Bakkour, the boy who lost his lower jaw during the random shelling on Baba Amr, and bled for more than seventy hours before losing his life. This inhumane scene has led a number of artists to reproduce the incident, including Khalil Younes, who largely remained true to the real nature of the scene, by depicting what was left from Hamza's face placed on top of a red-coloured space.

As for Amjad Wardeh[35], he chose the square to draw the upper part of Hamza's face on one side and the injured part on another, thus giving the viewer the option of either looking at the upper part or the lower one, or even at both together. This choice resembles the idea of a game and implies a sort of mockery of death. In a work entitled *Hamzeh Bakkour* (2012), Khaled Al Khani draws a face with no clear features, similar to his previous works, but in an emotional gesture adds red strikes to it in an attempt to reflect the tragedy of the real scene. Contrary to the previously mentioned works, this face does not necessarily bear any resemblance to the real picture of Hamzeh's face. However, entitling it after Hamzeh is a direct documentation of the incident and a reminder to the viewer of this child's suffering.

---

[35] Born in Damascus in 1984, Amjad Wardeh studied oil painting in the Faculty of Fine Arts, Damascus in 2007 and participated in various group exhibitions and contests. He was one of the winners of the "Made in MED" competition of Euromed Audiovisual for his film *War on Famous Canvas* 2014, which was featured in Cannes Film Festival (2014).

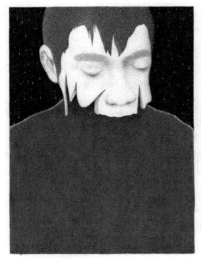 

Painting by Khalil Younes   Painting by Amjad Wardeh
Reprinted with kind permission

Khaled Al Khani, *Hamzeh Bakkour* (2012). Reprinted with kind permission.

In his movie entitled *His Name was Hamzeh Bakkour*, Dani Abou Louh (1983–) divides the image into two parts: on top, a steady picture of the unharmed part of the child's face, and on the changing bottom, we could see in pictures and videos various possibilities and expressions of the shape of his mouth. After an introduction explaining Hamzeh's story, Abou Louh starts the movie with a scene of a woman's mouth wearing lipstick, followed by several other scenes. In this film, the artist resorts to the montage technique, somehow similar to "collage" on a canvas, where pictures and videos of the lower part superpose. Similar to Amjad Wardeh's work, the film also radiates a playful nature.

Some of the works produced during the revolution can be seen as immortalisations of persons who lost their lives during the war and became symbols in time. One clear example of this is Waseem Marzouki's[36] work, *Tribute to the Soul of the Martyr Ghiath Matar*(2012), where in the upper part lies a dead head over a blood stain that occupies almost the entire canvas. What Marzouki depicts in this painting does not resemble what the martyr of the peaceful movement Ghiath Matar had looked like. However, as with Al Khani's work, specifying Matar's name in the title gives the dead body a definition, thus documenting his death.

Waseem Marzouki, *Tribute to the Soul of the Martyr* Ghiath Matar (2012).
Reprinted with kind permission.

---

[36] Born in Al Tabqa, Al Raqqa, in 1982, Waseem Marzouki graduated from the Visual Communication Department at the Faculty of Fine Arts in Damascus in 2007. He pursued his education at the Global Cinematography Institute in Hollywood, California, and took part in several exhibitions, the last of which was at Al Markhiya Gallery in Qatar, where he currently lives. He was awarded the Silver Simorgh at the Fajr International Film Festival, Tehran, in 2011.

Moreover, in a work by Tarek Butayhi[37], *The Martyr Child Oula Jablawi*, a girl's dead body is portrayed over a cold white mass. Traces of blood are spattered on her tiny head, while she raises her hand declaring her surrender to death. The work holds a clear emotional charge translated in the swift strokes of the brush. In this instance, too, the work's title identifies and somehow documents the dead body.

This approach is by no means an exception and is far from being uncommon in the history of art. In fact, in their work, artists have long documented and paid tribute to martyrs and the dead. What is peculiar here, however, is that the works named after the martyrs are produced immediately after their death and posted directly on social media, an approach not dissimilar to visual recordings. It is as if, unconsciously, the artist does not want these names to be forgotten.

Painting by Tarek Butayhi. Reprinted with kind permission.

---

[37] Born in Al Maliha, Damascus Countryside, in 1982, Tarek Butayhi graduated from the Oil Painting Department atthe Faculty of Fine Arts in Damascus in 2006. Women are the main topic in his work. He has participated in several group and solo exhibitions, the last of which took place in Art on 56th Gallery, Beirut, where he currently lives.

Various works were also produced under the title 'martyr' or 'martyrs', without specifying names or towns. One example is another piece by Tarek Butayhi, in which the dead body lies on a white space, as in the previous painting, with the amputated lower limbs adding further violence to the overall scene.

Two works by Youssef Abdelke are also worth mentioning in this regard. The first, *Father and Child* (2012), depicts a sad girl throwing herself on the dead body of her slaughtered father, lying in the middle of the canvas, dividing it into two quasi-equal parts. It is a scene rendered almost familiar in daily Syrian life. On the girl's side, we can see traces of red stains, representing blood, which distinguishes this work from most of Abdelke's other productions, where only black and white prevail.

As for the second work, *The Martyr's Mother* (2014), a woman in a black cape stands watchful before our eyes, putting her hands together and looking at us. Next to her, a mass of her size stands erect. It is indeed a recently-built tomb with an arched tombstone that reads the *Fatiha*[38] in a big font, with the phrase "Here lies the body of the deceased Mohammad Said Abd Al Rahman Al Shahbandar" written in Arabic in a smaller font. Both the woman and the tomb are of the same size, as if the artist is assimilating the living to the dead.

---

[38] Al Fatihah is the first chapter (surah) of the Quran. Its seven verses are a prayer for the guidance, lordship and mercy of God. This chapter has an essential role in Islamic prayer and is amongst other ritual uses, recited for the dead.

Youssef Abdelke, *The Martyr's Mother* (2014). Reprinted with kind permission.

It seems that the artist's interest has not changed much over the last few years. In fact, the topic of death prevails in Abdelke's works,

154

whether the dead body as seen in the first work, or the buried body in the second.

Several works of Syrian artists fall under the category of celebrating the dead body or martyr and have titles pertaining to the idea of martyrdom or death. This can be observed for example in works such as the *Martyr's Notebooks* collection by Ismail Rifai (1967–), *Pain* by Abdul Karim Majdal Al Beik, as well as the *Syrian Fear* collection by Ghylan Al Safadi (1977–), the *Cocoon* collection by Walid Al Masri (1979–), the *Revolution* collection by Khalil Younes and the *Miniatures of Syrian Death* by Omran Younes[39].

In *Miniatures of Syrian Death*, the dead child's body dominates the collection (produced in 2013 and 2014) and appears like a grave open to the spectators. In one of these works, a box is depicted with two dogs on top, looking in the same direction and barking, guarding the dead. Inside the box/tomb lies a baby's little body, hands extended and feet in the air as if playing. Is he buried in the painting exactly as he was killed, or did the artist imagine him both dead and playing? On the skull, a phosphoric stain lights up the grey-black colour occupying the painting. Traces of bullets pierce the surface of the paper, simulating the holes in the walls caused by snipers. "Oh death, who are thou? How could thou be this Syrian and omnipresent, yet remain to us ambiguous and unknown?"[40]

Third – The Fragmented Body

Representing the incomplete body or parts of it in artworks is usually an expression of the intense state of violence that accompanies the production of art pieces depicting such scenes. For this reason, this representation has become all the more common in Syrian artworks with the exacerbation of violence in the country. The decapitated head, for instance, did not have a strong presence at the beginning of the revolution, but with the rampant violence—including widespread

---

[39]   Born in Al Hasakah in 1971, Omran Younis graduated from the Photography Department at the Faculty of Fine Arts in Damascus in 1998 and obtained his Master's degree in the same major in 2000. He has participated in several group and solo exhibitions, the last of which was at Europia Art Gallery, Paris, in 2014.

[40]   From the text of Omran Younes' exhibition, Europia Art Gallery, Paris, 2014.

images and videos of Islamists decapitating heads—it became a clear theme, one that is common between several artists.

In *Head on a Plate* (2012), as the title suggests, artist Fadi Yazigi places a decapitated head on a plate, reminiscent of scenes of John the Baptist's decapitated head. This work, produced at the outset of the revolution, carries a symbolic value with a religious reference, and the artist revisits this theme one year later, in an even more shocking sculpture entitled *Tree* (2013), where a small tree carries decapitated heads instead of fruits; a scene where both violence and mockery meet.

In an engraving by Yaser Al Safi entitled *A Room with Millions of Walls* (2012), the artist randomly disperses several heads in an ambiguous space, rendered by the lines drawn in its upper part to a corner of a room, with traces of a previous drawing that has been erased. The title is inspired from that of a poetry collection by the late Mohammad Al Maghout[41], noting that the space refers somehow to a prison.

Yaser Al Safi, *A Room with Millions of Walls* (2012). Reprinted with kind permission.

---

[41] Mohammad Al Maghout (1934–2006), was a renowned Syrian poet, essayist and playwright, known for his fierce criticism of Arab governments.

In a more recent work by Yaser Al Safi entitled *The General Smokes* (2013), the decapitated head reemerges. This time, the artist chooses to place two human heads, one on top of the other, separated by open scissors that symbolise the state of cutting. On the right side, we can see the General: fat, on alert, and raising his hand to take the cigar out of his mouth. On the other side there are two sheep heads, directly under which there is a boxer which might symbolise the jailor. In this work, Al Safi equates human beings with sheep: slaughtering sheep is no different than slaughtering a human being in the Syrian scene of violence.

Also in a work by Omran Younes, the decapitated head appears on a box. On the forehead, we can see traces of bleeding caused by a gun shot. Here, too, the box brings to mind a previous work by Youssef Abdelke, where he depicts the decapitated head of a fish opening its mouth inside a wooden box.

The decapitated head is featured in later works by Youssef Abdelke as well, such as *Morning Star* (2013), where the head wearing a woolen hat is completely decapitated, with viscid blood running from the decapitation area. Above the head, on the upper part of the painting, a sentence is written in colloquial Arabic: "Oh Morning Star, you rose above Syria, you took away the good people and left the bad ones."

Forth – The Monstrous Body

The monstrous body has appeared in art production during the revolution as a particular topic, manifested as a sort of mockery of power and its symbols, as well as of the social phenomena reflecting these dynamics. One such example is the *Shabih*[42], a subject that emerged at the outset of the revolution and was later on included in the works of various artists. Azad Hamo[43], for example, illustrated this in his piece

---

[42] Shabih, pl. Shabiha: armed supporters of the Syrian regime; they are accused not only of killing and beating people who attend demonstrations, but also of carrying out campaigns of intimidation that have included executions, drive-by shootings and sectarian attacks.

[43] Born in 1979, Azad Hamo graduated from the Faculty of Fine Arts in Damascus in 2003 and has participated in several solo and group exhibitions, including Reemo Gallery in Venice, Italy, in 2012 and Amna Suraka Museum in Kurdistan, Iraq, in 2013. He was awarded at the Sanaa International Forum for Visual arts, Yemen in 2009. He currently lives in Italy.

entitled *Shabih*, (2012), in which a bearded head is wearing sunglasses, one of the common features of intelligence service members. The beard is thick and the face's colour is bluish, making it more akin to a monster.

Azad Hamo, *Shabih* (2012). Reprinted with kind permission.

In a work by Akram Al Halabi of the same title, an eerie body is depicted, with a black halo instead of a head, surrounded by a fine black line. A hand sticks out from the middle of this creature's body and is slightly bent downwards. Here, the monster is an imagined form of the *Shabih*, one that is quite abstract in nature.

Akram Al Halabi, *Shabih*. Reprinted with kind permission.

In Tarek Butayhi's *Shabiha*[44] (2012), the artist chooses to depict together a man's body, represented by a soldier wearing a helmet, turning his head towards us with a terrifying look while carrying a white pistol in his hand. There is also a female's body wearing a red dress, raised to show the figure's underwear and her thin pink legs. Butayhi is obviously mocking the idea of *Shabih*, assimilating it to a clown. This is reiterated by the bright colours chosen for the Shabiha outfit, in contrast

---

[44] Plural of shabih

with the dark black background that, despite the mockery, still reminds us of the event's tragedy.

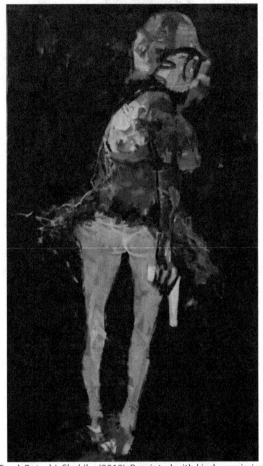

Tarek Butayhi, *Shabiha* (2012). Reprinted with kind permission.

In the recent works of Sabhan Adam which, similarly to previous ones, celebrate the monstrous body, the artist adds the military uniform to his creatures. Introducing the military uniform to his paintings comes as a result of the impact that all the changes occurring in society have had on the artist, and represents, in a way, a state of objection to the militarisation of society.

Fifth – The Political Monster

Numerous works ridicule the symbols of power, especially the president, turning them into monsters. Most of these works are digital and include posters or photomontages. The most distinguished one might be a portrait by Hani Charaf (1977–) of Bashar Al Assad, shrunk from both sides so as to narrow the forehead. The face appears to be one-eyed, similar to the Cyclops from Greek mythology, a mythical creature expressing rejection of civilisation, having no traditions or customs, as described by Homer[45]. This monster was in fact believed to be a skilled craftsman who forged weapons for the Gods.

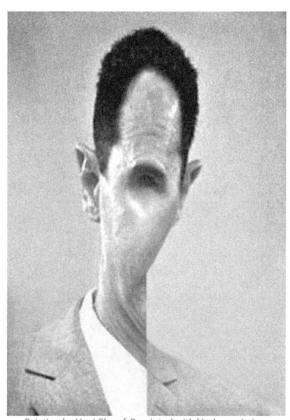

Painting by Hani Charaf. Reprinted with kind permission.

---

[45]   Guédron,Martial, *Monstres: Merveilles et créatures fantastiques*, Edition Hazan, Paris, 2011, P. 88.

In visual arts, however, there are no outstanding works addressing this particular matter, except for those of Monif Ajaj[46], who produced a collection of portraits distorting the details of Bashar Al Assad's face and exaggerating his features, so as to create further resemblance to a monster. These works are highly similar to caricatures in terms of exaggeration of details and traits, albeit uncategorised as such.

It is worth noting that the artist has previously produced works addressing this specific topic, such as *Arab Tyrants* (2012), where he introduced the idea of the political monster, bringing together the bodies of four former Arab leaders who were toppled by revolutions in their respective countries: the former Tunisian president Zine Al Abidin Ben Ali, his hand placed on his chest, as was his signature gesture, standing next to his Egyptian counterpart Hosni Mubarak and former Libyan leader Colonel Muammar Gaddafi, who in turn has his hand on the head of former Yemeni president, Ali Abdullah Saleh, who is depicted in a dark colour, referring to the burning traces inspired by his assassination attempt. The bodies are intertwined and similar in terms of their voluminous bloated paunches, forming what looks like a four-headed monster. The deliberate exaggeration and deformation intended for satirical purposes bring the work closer to the concept of "grotesque".

---

[46]   Born in Deir ez-Zor in 1967, Monif Ajaj graduated from the Belarusian State Academy of Art in 1995. He has participated in several solo and group exhibitions, the last of which was a joint (group?) exhibition in Bordeaux, France. He currently lives in France.

Monif Ajaj, *Arab Tyrants* (2012). Reprinted with kind permission.

Sixth – The Hybrid Body

The hybrid body has also been remarkably present in the works produced during the revolution. In fact, Syrian artists have relied on an imagination that is not short on mockery, in order to create funny creatures. This can be seen in the latest works of Maher Al Baroudi, where the sheep, a main topic for the artist, anthropomorphises, or perhaps where a human zoomorphises.

In a work by Khaled Takriti (1964–) entitled *Photocopies* (2013), a man stands in the middle of the scene lifting his hand to wear a glove, while his face is completely hidden behind the mask of an angry bull. On both sides, we can see duplicate figures that present several possibilities for one character, combining the laughing head of a chicken with a human body, a character inspired from billboards. There seems to be no clear rapport between the subjects of this painting, except for the fact that they are reproducing each other, morphing into hybrid and funny creatures.

Khaled Takriti, *Photocopies* (2013). Reprinted with kind permission.

Artist Fadi Al Hamwi[47] touches upon the hybrid body by placing a donkey's head on a human body wearing a uniform, a piece reminiscent of Maher Al Baroudi's work during the late nineties, where animals replaced the human element, in a style not far from mockery. Apparently, the visual reference goes back to the works of Spanish artist Francisco Goya in his collection *Los Caprichos*, where animals incarnate human appearances as a sort of mockery of a society in decay.

In another work by Fadi Al Hamwi entitled *Syrian Global Warming* (2013), we see the body of a strange creature whose appearance is shaped by a series of coloured strikes, dominated by black, within the form of a body. The face is wearing a protective mask and the shape appears over a background of bright colours, mainly sky blue.

In another work by the same artist entitled *Bathroom Mirror* (2014), the concept of the hybrid body is unmistakable: a cow gazing at its

---

[47] Born in Damascus in 1986, Fadi Al Hamwi graduated from the Oil Painting Department at the Faculty of Fine Arts, Damascus University, in 2010. He has participated in several group exhibitions, in addition to various workshops and contemporary art and multimedia exhibitions. He also has presented several installations and "video art" works in Damascus and Beirut, where he currently lives.

reflection in the mirror is standing on two human feet, one of which is bandaged. Through the cow's torso, the bones are visible, as if we are looking at an X-ray. Al Hamwi has in fact used the X-ray idea in several previous works, in an endeavor to go beyond all that is visible and hidden in both the human and animal appearances, not only physically, but psychologically as well.

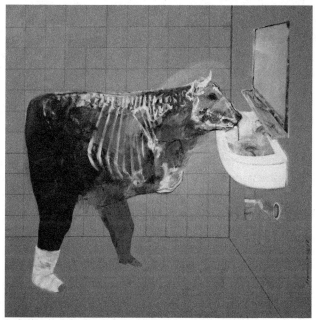

Fadi Al Hamwi, *Bathroom Mirror* (2014). Reprinted with kind permission.

In this work, the face bleeds on the sink in the bathroom, depicted by lines drawn of porcelain squares dividing the background. Some similarities can be pinpointed with the works of artist Francis Bacon, in terms of the suggested space, unit ambiance and isolation. The concept of the monster might not be expressive of the hideous war as much as it reflects an individual state stemming from a personal concern. Al Hamwi says, "I try to incite the viewer by connecting to the animal body, incarnating its status and identifying with it, regardless of its cruelty. The general concept addresses acts of violence that are not directly felt and touched in our lives, and sheds light on the sharpness of instincts and on how to incite sentiments of fear in them, revealing the dark side that all of us humans have"[48].

The idea of the animal, particularly the hybrid one, has always been a special feature in the recent works of Fadi Al Hamwi. In addition to the aforementioned pieces, the artist has produced a collection of works depicting humanised dinosaurs; we see for instance a dinosaur riding a bicycle or a wedding of two dinosaurs. All of these are funny scenes with a symbolic dimension. They celebrate an extinct animal species and perhaps presage the extinction of mankind. Naturally, all of these works, despite being funny, harbor implicit violence.

Creatures in fiction, myths and jinn stories have long scared us and stimulated our imagination: half-human, half-animal creatures, humans turning into animals or monsters dressed like humans, etc. With the symbolic dimensions they represent, these monsters constitute a visual supply of material that the artist draws from for inspiration. However, the references are not limited to stories, as some artists have borrowed expressions of the monster from western movies in order to showcase the daily state of terror in their country.

In a work by Mohannad Orabi[49] from his *It's No Longer About Me* (2012) series, we see a face looking at us. Its gender is hard to determine and its eyes are shining, similarly to most of the artist's recent works, whereas the eyes in his previous works were all black, without any sparkle. The black robe and the hair are embroidered with decorative plant prints, as if intended to attenuate the roughness of the "mask" element added to the face. The red mask in this case reminds us of that of Dr. Hannibal Lecter[50], a character from *The Silence of the Lambs*. The mask in the painting is represented as a vital part of the face, coloured in grey by the artist, bringing it one step closer to the dead. The reason Orabi has borrowed this character is because it is a

---

[48]   Mohammad Omran, *Interview with Fadi Al Hamwi,*[s.n], [s.l.], 2015.

[49]   Born in Damascus in 1977, Mohannad Orabi graduated from the Faculty of Fine Arts in Damascus, Oil Painting Department, in 2000. He was awarded the first prize in the Young Artists Exhibition in Damascus. He has participated in several solo and group exhibitions. He currently lives in Dubai.

[50]   Hannibal Lecter is a character of a cannibal psychiatrist who has been locked down in a psychiatric facility and forced to wear the mask for fear of biting like wild animals.

famous one, which makes it easier to showcase the barbaric situation invading the Syrian society.

Painting by Mohannad Orabi. Reprinted with kind permission.

In conclusion, we can say that there is a wide variety of techniques used in tackling the topic of the monstrous body, which, if anything, refers to the exacerbated situation in Syrian society.

Conclusion

After this extensive look at some of the artworks produced during the revolution in Syria, we can say that they essentially celebrate the element of the dead body. It is true that this subject is not uncommon on the art scene; however, it has generally been defined as an act of solidarity with national causes. For instance, the idea of the martyr, the most prominent manifestation of the subject/theme of the dead body, was primarily related to the Palestinian cause, whereas today, this idea has been expanded so as to become Syrian par excellence. Nevertheless, several artists who were previously known for being committed to a political cause ceased their production during the revolution, while many others who would never have described themselves in the past as being committed to specific political causes have started producing works that reflect their relationship with the revolution and the recent developments in Syria. This applies, for example, to artists Randa Maddah, Tarek Butayhi, Khalil Younes, Amjad Wardeh, Tammam Azzam, Abdalla Omari, Ghylan Al Safadi, Omran Younes, Abdul Karim Majdal Al Beik and many others.

If we exclude Maher Al Baroudi's works from the eighties, in which the vagrant is depicted as a dead body on the sidewalk, the element of the dead body as a result of natural causes is absent from pre- and post-revolution artworks, indicating that the Syrian artistic experiences still perceive death as a highly-valued symbolic state that is far from ordinary or natural.

Post-revolution images depicting the dead body are noticeably more violent than pre-revolution ones. This could be due to artists' reliance on photos and videos circulating over the Internet, something which was not widely available in the past. For this reason, we could say that former experiences were generally more symbolic, in contrast with the straightforward, almost blunt nature of current artworks. However, the concept of body art remains largely absent from the work of Syrian artists, as they have yet to consider their bodies as tools for a direct, forthright artwork. We might exclude from this some artistic performances, such as those presented by Hiba Al Ansari or Iman Hasbani, but there are no examples of more direct experiences as in

Western art. It seems that the relationship between Syrian artists and the body remains limited, generally speaking, to expressing themselves through their paintings.

Most of the works containing images of the dead body bear the name of the martyr and indicate the location of the scene, something which has not changed before and after the revolution. Examples of this are *A Woman from Douma*, *A Martyr from Daraa*, *I am from Syria*, *Karm Al Zaytoun*, etc. These works have a documentary aspect, as they refer to a specific incident or massacre, which is not new to the Syrian art repertoire, but which has now simultaneously become more intensified and localised. Despite the presence of the grotesque in some cases, which indicates a state of criticism, most works remain inclined towards lamentational seriousness.

The fragmented body, especially the decapitated head, is strongly present in post-revolution works, whereas previously this element could only be found in specific past experiences, such as *Guillotine* by Mustafa Ali in 2010. Today, it can be seen in the works of Yaser Al Safi, Fadi Yazigi, Youssef Abdelke, Omran Younes and many others.

The elements of the monstrous and grotesque body can be increasingly found in post-revolution works, particularly the young generation's productions, as there is a noticeable inclination toward exploring new "post-human" shapes, or shapes that are parallel to the human being. In general, this translates the state of concern and worry imposed by the status-quo. In fact, the monster as a concept expresses, in one way or another, a state of unconscious fear, a fear of the extinction of the human species perhaps. Most works in this category fall under the concept of the hybrid body, which combines human and animal elements.

In the past, the topic of the monster was not featured in Syrian visual art, except for some cases as in works by Youssef Abdelke and Maher Al Baroudi. There were undeniably various works of highly expressive value, but they can be differentiated from the idea of the monster, as they only rely on the exaggeration of human body parts, while the monster in general suggests a shape and appearance that is completely different from that of a human being.

The sick body is only present in some specific experiences, such as that of Maher Al Baroudi, who produced a collection of works simulating psychological illness in the eighties and nineties. Some other experiences, such as the works of Fadi Al Hamwi based on the idea of an X-ray of humans and animals, could reflect certain aspects of this topic. However, it is hard to place these works under the category of the sick body, as they are rather closer to the monstrous body.

It is still very early to discuss about the impact of the imagined image on the collective memory in light of the real and escalating daily violence in Syria. In the long term, perhaps, we might refer back to the imagined image to point out to a certain event, such as a massacre for example. The intensity and widespread use of "raw" real images could be helpful in this regard, as it might lead in the future to favor the use of the "symbolic" imagined image, using it as a visual reference of the real incident. This does not mean that the mission of artistic work should be limited to alleviating the horror of real violence or to merely documenting the incident, but to create, in one way or another, a parallel image of a specific incident in the collective imagination. *Hama 30* by Khalil Younes is a great example of this attitude.

The imagined image might also serve to fill the visual void and replace the prevailing image. The "stereotypical" image of the martyr could thus take on new forms, owing to the works of artists who have dealt with this topic, as can be seen in *A Martyr from Daraa* or *Mother of the Martyr* by Youssef Abdelke, *The Martyr* by Tarek Butayhi, etc.

Most of the artworks produced during the revolution were keen on triggering a sense of shock similar to the one caused by real-life violence. The changes that have occurred in Syria over the past four years have very likely led to certain transformations in the relationship between the artist and the Syrian cause, as well as in artists' relationship with their tools, creative production and surrounding reality.

After this brief review of some of the works of Syrian artists tackling the subject of the tormented body, we can say that most artists have pursued their artistic path without breaking with their past experiences. Despite the wide variety of methods used to represent violence, the dead body has remained the central element in the majority of these experiences over the past four years.

Sources and References

Arabic Books

AALLOUN Abdel Aziz, *The sixties' twist in the contemporary art history in Syria*, House of Culture, Damascus, 2003.

ELIAS Marie, KASSAB HASSAN Hanan, *Dictionary of Theatre: Terms and Concepts of Drama and the Performing Arts*, Librairie du Liban, Beirut, 1997.

OMRAN Mohammad, *Maher Al Baroud between two cultures, how can we analyse his work?* (Master thesis), Lyon II University, France, 2009.

Accompanying text for the exhibition of the visual artist Omran Younes, Europe Gallery, Paris, 2014.

English Books

BUSSAGLI Marco, *Le corps anatomie et symboles*, Editions Hazan Paris, 2006.

Eco Umberto, *Histoire de la beauté*, Edition Flammarion, Paris, 2004.

MICHALOWSKI Kazimiers, *L'art de l'Égypte*, Paris, éditions CITADELLES & MAZENOD-EDITIO, 1968/1994 (Nouvelle Edition Revenu et Augmentée par Jean-Pierre Corteggiani Alessandro Roccati).

Onfray Michel, *Catalogue Vladimir Velickovic—Blessure(s)*, Fondation Coprim, Paris, 2002.

O'Reilly Sally, *Le corps dans l'art contemporain*, Edition Thames et Hudson, Paris, 2010.

Présentation de Jean-Pierre Dhainault, GOYA LES CAPRICES, Paris, Les éditions de l'Amateur, 2005.

ROBERTS-JONES, Philippe, *Daumier Mœurs Conjugales*, (préface, catalogue et notices), Edition Vilo, Paris, 1967.

Electronic References

Art. Liberty. Syria Facebook page
https://www.facebook.com/Art.Liberte.Syrie?fref=ts

Creative Memory http://www.creativememory.org/?lang=ar

Interviews

Interview with Nawal Al Ali, Al Akhbar Lebanese newspaper, issue number 268, Beirut, 2007.

Mohammad Omran, *Interview with Fadi Al Hamwi,*[s.n], [s.l.], 2015.

Mohammad Omran, *Interview with Maher Al Baroudi*, [s.l.], [s.n], 2008.

Mohammad Omran, *Interview with Shada Al Safadi*, [s.l.], [s.n], 2012.

Mohammad Omran

Born in Damascus in 1979. He studied sculpture in the Faculty of Fine Arts in Damascus where he also taught from 2005 till 2007. He holds a master's degree in history of contemporary arts from Lyon 2 University. He participated in many solo and collective exhibitions in Syria, Egypt, Jordan, Kuwait, Lebanon, Turkey, Belgium, Denmark, France, Germany and the United States. He also published articles about visual arts in many newspapers. He lives and works in Paris.

Children in the Shadow
of the Islamic State:
Jihadi Schooling and Recruitment

Prepared by: Wasim Raif Al Salti
Supervised by: Jamal Chehayed
Research paper conducted in 2015–2016

Summary

Despite the fact that most Syrian and Iraqi children have been subjected to physical and emotional harm and violence due to the ongoing wars in both countries, some of them are now living under the dangerous rule of the self-proclaimed caliphate of the so-called 'Islamic State'. While the organisation controls thousands of square kilometres from Raqqa in Syria to Mosul in Iraq—a land with an abundance of oil fields, arms warehouses, historical monuments, museums, wealth and banks — the true wealth of IS is the children under its rule. These children are as much of a wealth for the organisation as they are a loss for Syrian and Iraqi societies.

Given the grave danger of child recruitment on children themselves and on humanity as a whole, and in parallel with the international and Arab fight against the organisation on both the military and media fronts, this research aims to expose the organisation's crimes against Syrian children and its violation of all their natural and legal rights. It also seeks to reveal how the organisation imposes harsh duties and obligations on children and subjects them to its hateful, violent and deadly ideology, by shedding light on different aspects of this phenomenon and attempting to paint an accurate and comprehensive picture of the propaganda and education to which children living under the rule of the extremist organisation have been subjected.

Among the difficulties faced during the course of this research is the lack of field studies on the situation of children living under the rule of IS, as well as the lack of statistics regarding the number of children who have died or who are fighting for the organisation, as the latter bans any such activity. The numbers provided by newspapers and research centres are mere estimates. The organisation itself does provide some figures through its websites and media outlets, such as the Al Furqan, Al Bayan, Aa'maq and Al Hayat news agencies. Other websites that support the organisation also offer some insight through the articles, studies, magazines and films they produce. Most of these websites, however, are constantly being hacked and reported by internet users who, by doing so, participate in the war on IS in their own way. This makes the use of such sources for research purposes extremely difficult most of the time.

Other sources and references include Western media outlets covering news about the organisation through numerous statements, articles and condemnations around child recruitment, as well as Arab media outlets and research centres that have published papers and articles about the same phenomenon. However, some of these sources only give a general description of the matter without delving into the details, while others focus only on one aspect of it, or achieve little more than expressing sympathy and denouncing the organisation's actions. Moreover, despite the dozens of books written about the formation, actions and ideology of IS, none of them focus on the phenomenon of child recruitment. For all these reasons, the only sources that provide insight on the situation of children under IS rule are those of the organisation itself. This coverage, however, is no doubt governed by the image that the organisation wants to paint of itself – an image that constitutes, in its own right, condemning evidence of the organisation's crimes against children, namely raising them from a very young age on the culture of hatred and violence.

The paper is divided into three parts. The first part recounts the emergence of IS and gives an overview of the situation of children under its rule. It describes how the organisation has treated children throughout the various periods of its existence. This part has also relied on the historical method, in addition to obtaining information from books and articles about this subject.

After the historical overview, the second part of the paper discusses children's education under the rule of IS in terms of mechanisms, characteristics and how children are groomed to be recruited in the organisation later on. Finally, the third part examines the techniques and methods of recruitment. The second and third parts of the paper are based on a series of studies, articles and publications from the organisation itself, as well as relevant videos. They also follow a descriptive approach in presenting and analysing information to arrive at results that show the effect that each of these grooming methods has on children's lives and their future. This descriptive-analytical approach allows us to better understand the phenomenon of child recruitment and to examine its educational, moral, religious and military aspects.

Thus, the goal of this paper is to give an idea of how IS teachings can transform a child, by examining the case of the so-called 'jihadi child'.

The research paper includes three appendices: the first states the number of children recruited by IS and those who have been killed; the second provides examples of statements issued by international organisations and institutions to denounce the actions of IS; and the third appendix lists key events in the history of IS.

Introduction

Since its emergence in 2006, the so-called Islamic State (IS) has exerted every effort to establish and expand its control in both Iraq and Syria through various means. Using a range of different strategies, from intimidation to enticement and targeted recruitment, IS has consistently deployed its full arsenal of available resources in order to maintain its hold and control.

By late 2014, IS had taken hold of considerable resources in the regions it controlled, spanning thousands of kilometres. In fact, by this time, "IS had seized the entire governorate of Al Raqqa, Mosul, the chemical weapons facility in Muthana, the city of Tal Afar and its strategic airbase, the Camp Speicher military base in Iraq—along with their existing oil fields, weapons depots, archaeological monuments and museums, funds and banks. But the chief asset of all remains the thousands of children."[1] Statistical estimates place the number of children recruited by IS at approximately 50,000[2] from the outset of recruitment until late 2016.

Given the danger posed by recruitment of any kind and that of children in particular, this paper aims to offer insight on this phenomena, as well as to expose the practices and behaviours of IS against children. While this paper mainly focuses on Syria, it will also look at the overall dynamics and issues in all IS-controlled territories. The study will examine and shed light on IS violations of the natural and legal rights of children, who are denied their right to a childhood and are subjected to gruelling obligations intended to cultivate a doctrine of hate, violence and death among children in its territories and beyond.

The paper also aims to unpack the specific and emerging phenomenon of child recruitment by IS through examination, analysis, and deduction, in order to illustrate how this approach has become a fully-

---

[1]   ISIS-held regions in Iraq and Syria [online source], Al Arabiya, available at: https://goo.gl/BIBLum, published on 3/3/2015, accessed on 1/4/2015

[2]   Sengupta. Kim, ISIS indoctrinating children to plan attacks on Big Ben, Eiffel Tower and Statue of Liberty, [online source], INDEPENDENT, available at: https://goo.gl/ptkfWK, accessed on 25/12/2015

fledged system through which IS has successfully recruited hundreds of children. The paper investigates the methods used by IS to achieve this by exploring the different aspects of this phenomenon and its internal dynamics. It identifies the means and methods that IS has used to formulate this system and ensure its success and survival. The paper also raises the following questions: how did the practices, behaviours and violations used by IS influence the ideas and way of life of the children exposed to them? What are the tools used by IS to enforce such practices? How effective are these tools in influencing children under IS control? How far do IS members go in terms of violence and extremism in both schooling and training camps to implant IS ideology in children with the aim of radicalising them?

In fact, all of these questions branch out from the paper's main question, which also introduces the main ideas and issues that will be discussed: how successful has IS been in grooming a generation that is fully committed to its ideology and culture? What are the negative and long-term impacts of the emergence of such a generation? Are we witnessing a transient strategy of recruitment that is inevitable in any armed conflict and that ultimately ends when the war draws to a close? Providing answers to these questions is a first step on the way to reach a comprehensive understanding and analysis of this recruitment phenomenon.

In terms of structure, the paper consists of three sections. The first section offers an overview of the emergence of IS, the status of children in territories under its control and how this has developed over the various phases of IS evolution and expansion. The second section explains the system of child recruitment created by IS, the essential components of which are indoctrination and schooling. The paper will examine critical changes introduced to basic schooling following the seizure of educational facilities and institutions. It will also look at how these changes have helped shape a new or emerging identity for children, setting them apart from their respective societies with new social references and, ultimately, paving the way for their recruitment. In the third section, the paper examines the approach of establishing training camps for children, in addition to how IS targets, attracts and engages children through games and contests using outreach activities in public spaces. This section will also discuss the military tasks assigned by IS to children and, finally, present the "jihadi character", through which one can understand the key identity traits of a child recruited by IS.

In the first section, the paper references published books and articles, as historical methodology for research and inquiry. In its second and third sections, the paper relies on analysis, comparison and deduction. This is in addition to the cross-checking of information and data from several sources, which is especially important given the lack of reliable field studies on the number of children, their educational, health and mental status, as well as the number of child casualties and combatants. To be sure, these numbers are difficult to obtain, as IS prohibits such field studies from being conducted. In fact, anyone who attempts to film, document or report on the situation in IS-controlled regions is tortured and potentially even killed.

Therefore, the paper researches and analyses the status of children living in IS-controlled territories using three types of sources of information. First, it resorts to reviewing and monitoring IS sources—this includes online IS pages, news outlets speaking on its behalf and websites sympathizing with it, and publishing its articles, studies, magazines and videos. The second source of information is writings and literature by scholars interested in radical organisations and/or individuals who have sought to uncover and expose IS practices, including former IS members who describe details and dynamics unknown to outsiders. The latest example of such material is a documentary entitled *Studio of Horror,* which aired on Al Arabiya channel in early February 2017. It was an investigative piece following in the footsteps of three former members of the IS propaganda team. The documentary reveals the state-of-the-art propaganda resources acquired by IS and the volume of funds devoted to the generation of IS propaganda. The third source of information is periodicals published by organisations monitoring children's rights, as well as media coverage from Arab and Western outlets that have addressed this subject.

Although IS has garnered considerable media coverage, attention and research worldwide, finding and examining these sources was no easy feat; most IS websites and the majority of its online propaganda material are routinely hacked into and reported by activists to shut them down to prevent them from disseminating their propaganda.

This has made finding and retrieving material for verification very diffi-cult more often than not.

The paper features three appendices that offer rich material for fur-ther reading on the phenomenon of IS recruitment. The first appendix illustrates the number of children recruited by IS and the number of those who have died. The second appendix gives a roundup of data and worldwide condemnations issued by global organisations and institutions. The third appendix highlights key events in the IS timeline.

It is the hope of this research paper to shed light on the dangers of such practices, which exploit children for political gain and deprive them of their most basic rights, while moulding a future generation that carries a radical ideology. The catastrophic repercussions of this phenomenon will be difficult to address without dismantling the very mechanisms that have produced it. That is the intended contribution of this paper, however modest it may be.

First – Historical Background of the Emergence of IS

This section presents the major events leading to the rise of IS in 2006 in Iraq, along with some of the reasons behind its emergence. It touches on the strategies adopted by IS to entrench its rule in the regions it controlled, including training camps for children, which IS had set up from the outset. This section also addresses the reasons that have motivated IS to continue to establish such camps, and how this has paved the way for subsequent activities aimed to recruit children, namely reliance on schooling to indoctrinate children with IS ideology.

1 – The Emergence of IS

Since its creation in 2006, the Islamic State has assumed three names: Islamic State of Iraq (ISI), which then morphed into the Islamic State of Iraq and Syria (ISIS)/Daesh, and later the Islamic State (IS), following its control of vast territories as of July 2014.

IS first appeared in 2006 in Iraq, under the leadership of Abu Omar Al Baghdadi[3] until his death in a US raid in 2010. He was succeeded by Abu Bakr Al Baghdadi. IS, as an organisation, was an offshoot of another, the Mujahedin Shura Council, created by Abu Omar Al Baghdadi at the order of Abu Musab Al Zarqawi[4], emir of Al Qaeda in Iraq (AQI). Al Zarqawi sought to unify jihadi organisations and factions operating in Iraq to have them serve under one common banner. Following Al Zarqawi's death on 8 June 2006, as a result of a US raid on his house in Baqouba, the members of the Mujahedin Shura Council and other jihadi brigades and groups present in Iraq[5] met under the then-called

---

[3] Hamid Daoud Al Zawi, claimed by his circle to be a direct descendant of Prophet Muhammad, he was close to Abu Musab Al Zarqawi. He joined Jama'at Al Tawhid wal-Jihad (Organisation of Monotheism and Jihad) founded by Al Arqawi in Iraq in 2002. He later became a member of the Mujahedin Shura Council, then emir of the organisation.

[4] Ahmad Fadil Nazzal Al Khalayla, born in Jordan in 1966, he pledged allegiance to Al Qaeda on 8 October 2004, after being emir of Jama'at Al Tawhid wal-Jihad.

[5] Some 12 brigades, 7 groups and several Sunni tribes attended the meeting at the time.

Mutayibin Coalition. The meeting issued a constituent statement for what was to become ISI on 15 October 15 2006, and pledged allegiance to Abu Omar Al Baghdadi as emir of the organisation.

Al Baghdadi proceeded to form a cabinet for the fledgling state and appointed its ministers. At the time, ISI controlled large swathes of territory, further expanded following the "pledge of allegiance of many members and tribes of the Sunni community in Iraqi governorates such as Saladin, Diyala, Anbar, Mosul, Babil, Wasit and Kirkuk."[6] The emerging power and appeal of IS at the time allowed it to establish a training camp for children. The organisation set up a camp, named The Birds of Paradise, on the banks of the Diyala River, Iraq, to train children between the ages of 9 and 15. Children were trained on how to kill in preparation to be suicide attackers. The first batch to graduate from the camp was a group of thirty children[7]. A defected Al Qaeda leader exposed the practices of The Birds of Paradise camp leader, a man by the name of Abu Jaber, at the time. Abu Jaber was "obsessed with raping young boys; the training programme depended on turning them into drug addicts before committing suicide."[8]

During this period of IS expansion and hegemony in 2006, the Iraqi government, in coordination with the US forces commanded by General David Petraeus, formed the so-called Awakening Army or Sons of Iraq (Sahawaat), whose ranks included fighters of all ages, to combat and liquidate IS wherever it existed in the regions of Iraq. The Awakening fighting force consisted of "100,000 fighters, well-trained at the hands of US military experts. The US also sent approximately 21,000 fighters to support the Awakening fighting forces."[9]

Once IS expansion was halted and its hegemony checked, the Iraqi parliament announced the Status of Forces Agreement on 27 November 2008, requiring the withdrawal of US troops from Iraqi cities on 30

---

[6]   Ibrahim. Fuad, *ISIS from Al Najdi to Al Baghdadi: Nostalgia for the Caliphate*, Awal Centre for Studies and Documentation, Beirut, 2015, p. 42

[7]   The figure appeared in: Abu Zeid. Adnan, *Birds of Paradise: Project of rape and explosive belts*, [online source], Iraqi Women's League – IWL, available at: https://goo.gl/TI8EsF, published on 30/5/2009, accessed on 3/3/2016

[8]   Ibrahim. Fuad, *ISIS from Al Najdi to Al Baghdadi*, op. cit., p. 45

[9]   Atwan. Abdel Bari, *The Islamic State: The Roots, the Savagery and the Future*, Dar al Saqi, Beirut, 2015, p. 86

June 2009, and from all Iraqi territory by the end of 2011.[10] Al Maliki's government "booted half of the Sons of Iraq's fighters, sending them to the street. It stopped paying their monthly wages which amounted to 300 US dollars (…) while the other half it kept on a leash of false promises."[11] As a result of such practices by Al Maliki's government, grudges welled up among these fighters—to the disproportionate advantage of IS. IS seized the opportunity to re-establish its popularity and reintegrate disillusioned or bitter Awakening fighters under its wing. It became active again and "on 19 August 2009, Baghdad awoke to a series of blasts, tallying 122 victims, which targeted the Ministries of Foreign Affairs and Finance. IS claimed responsibility for the blasts, after the Iraqi government had declared the capital city of Baghdad as part of the green zone, which was highly fortified and classified as safe."[12]

IS activity and attacks against Iraqi government forces directly impacted children in Iraq, especially attacks or clashes that broke out between 2006 and 2008, resulting in grave damage. A report published by the Global Network for Rights and Development (GNRD) details the magnitude of the harm inflicted upon the children of Iraq. "Damages have been estimated at approximately 5,000,000 orphans, the majority of whom experienced dire and complicated social circumstances. Moreover, 30% of children under the age of 17 in Iraq could not sit for their final school examinations. The passing rate in official exams did not exceed 40% of all students sitting for the exams in the country."[13]

IS presence gradually declined in Iraq following a series of defeats and the depletion of its forces in successive wars between 2006 and 2011, until the beginning of the Syrian uprising. IS leader Abu Bakr Al Baghdadi decided to send a number of his soldiers to Syria to directly participate in the uprising. He chose for this mission Abu Mohammad

---

[10]   Atwan. Abdel Bari, *The Islamic State*, ibid., p. 86
[11]   Atwan. Abdel Bari, *The Islamic State*, ibid., p. 82
[12]   Atwan. Abdel Bari, *The Islamic State*, ibid., p. 84
[13]   *Iraq: Children between harsh present and unknown future*, [online source], Child Rights International Network (CRIN) website, available at https://goo.gl/ZwUfKg, published on 28/9/2008, accessed on 10/1/2016

Al Julani,[14] "since Al Julani had already pledged allegiance to Al Bagh-dadi and fought under his command in Iraq before relocating to Syria and establishing an IS branch there under the name of Jabhat Al Nusra Li Ahl el Sham (Nusra Front), all with financial and military support from Al Baghdadi."[15] Abu Mohammad Al Julani proposed to Abu Bakr Al Baghdadi "a project for jihad in Syria. Abu Bakr authorised and en-trusted him to proceed, as the commander of the Nusra Front in Syria. On 24 January 2012, Al Julani issued a statement in which he declared the establishment of the Nusra Front, which would become, on 28 July 2016, Jabhat Fateh Al Sham and later Jabhat Tahrir Al Sham after it was proscribed as a terrorist organisation."[16]

In Syria, IS did not spare children as it emerged and allied itself with Nusra. In fact, its recruitment of children in Syria was more organised and systematic than it had been in Iraq. IS immediately began setting up da'awa (outreach) caravans in public squares under its control, dis-tributing presents, toys and sweets to the children who would crowd around the caravans. IS would then "urge them to jihad and mobilisa-tion, attended by the blasting of proselytising and rallying songs which IS typically used in its visual propaganda."[17] Such activities and events orchestrated by IS to attract children were neither coincidence nor circumstantial; rather, they were based on intentional strategies that were carefully designed and articulated by recruitment officers.

---

[14] Known by the nom de guerre Abu Mohammad Al Julani, he was born in 1981 in the town of Al Shiheil, part of the city of Deir Al Zor, to a family that originally hailed from the governorate of Idlib. He was openly affiliated with the Salafi-jihadi movement, especially Al Qaeda which he joined in Iraq after the US invasion in 2003. He operated under the command of deceased leader Abu Musab Al Zarqawi and later his successors. He still vows allegiance to Al Qaeda leader Ayman Al Zawahiri, and acts according to his guidance and instructions.

[15] Ibrahim. Fuad, ISIS from Al Najdi to Al Baghdadi, op. cit., p. 123

[16] Amro. Abu Sefian; Al Kradsi, Sadat; Al Noubi, Abu Ziad Muhammad Yaqoub, The Real Islamic State…ISIS: Documented Sayings of Group Emirs and Leaders, [n.p], [n.d], p. 18

[17] Details of the full operation: how children are recruited into ISIS ranks, [online source], Orient Net, available at: https://goo.gl/MlteVp, published on 25/7/2015, accessed on 1/3/2016

2 – IS Strategies for Entrenching Its Rule in IS-Held Regions

The first real threat to children in IS-controlled areas emerged in late 2013, with the creation of the first IS training camp to recruit children in Syria under the name of Al Zarqawi Cubs.[18] This happened in parallel with other measures taken by IS, exposing children to its ideology and encouraging them to emulate its actions, starting from early childhood and extending into schooling, rather than focusing on the recruitment of young adults.

The measures undertaken by IS concerning educational institutions and curricula demonstrate the importance IS placed on children, in that it facilitated the packaging and delivery of IS ideology to them. Moreover, IS saw this as an opportunity to support and facilitate the recruitment of children, by introducing them to the organisation itself, followed by praxis, i.e. recruitment. Upon assuming control over an area, IS would first shut down all the schools, then declare a redesign of the old curricula, which the organisation immediately condemned as heresy and vestiges of the old regime. IS proclaimed that anyone who disobeyed or disregarded its teachings risked death under the serious charge of treason. The second section of the paper (Schooling in IS Territories), will address, in detail, the changes made to the educational system under IS rule. It will also describe the capacity of IS to implement a method specifically designed for targeting and recruiting children.

Intimidation remains the primary strategy adopted by IS whenever it acquires control of a new territory. This approach was evident when IS seized the Iraqi governorate of Mosul in June 2014, when "two brigades of the Iraqi army surrendered their weapons, nearly half a million Mosul residents fled, and IS executed 670 Shiite prisoners and 13 mosque imams."[19]

Intimidation as a strategy was inspired by several sources, often referenced by IS leaders. The main source is a book entitled *Manage-*

---

[18] Refer to the video report: *ISIS creates Al Zarqawi Cubs camp, violates child rights and international conventions*, [online source], Al Jadeed channel, available at: https://goo.gl/0FzQ93, published on 12/4/2014, accessed on 2/2/2016
[19] Atwan. Abdel Bari, *The Islamic State*, ibid., p. 38

ment of Savagery: The Most Critical Stage through Which the Islamic Nation Will Pass[20] by Abu Bakr Naji, who has been a controversial figure since 2003, following the US invasion of Iraq. At that time, there were several claims that he was a fabrication, a fictional character. However, several books and numerous researches on Al Qaeda and IS have confirmed the actual existence of Abu Bakr Naji. Fuad Ibrahim, a researcher focusing on jihadi organisations, goes as far as to say, in his book *ISIS from Al Najdi to Al Baghdadi*, that Naji was a prominent Al Qaeda theorist, nicknamed Al Sheikh. His name was Seif Al Adl and was originally from Palestine.

Ibrahim describes the book as one of the chief architectural texts for jihadi groups on military planning and tactics, as well as on the managing and distribution of roles and responsibilities among their members. This explains why IS has resorted to the action plan laid out in the book. Indeed, despite the fact that the text is old, as the writer suggests in the introduction to the book, its pages illuminate the complete strategy of IS, which has built its foundations over three stages.

Sheikh Naji calls the first stage "Spite and Exhaustion". Here, the primary tasks that a member should undertake is to assault the enemy using attack and retreat tactics, followed by a siege to exhaust the enemy economically, socially and psychologically. This phase allows the use of all available means—including killings and violence—for the purpose of exhausting the enemy.

Once organisation members complete the attack and retreat operations, the area can then be subjected to the so-called 'management of savagery'. Savagery occurs when the area or society descends into political chaos causing social insecurity. Under such circumstances, amid the absence of the power and authority responsible for protecting and managing its various services, including health and education, it becomes necessary to manage the rampant savagery and chaos, even if the means to do so is savagery in and of itself, or even excessive use of violence. Savagery thus becomes the only way to subject an area to a new rule. Finally, in the third stage (Enabling and Establishing Islamic Rule and an Islamic State), the organisation's sleeper cells in the target area are unleashed.

---

[20] Abu Bakr. Naji, *Management of Savagery: The Most Critical Stage through which the Islamic Nation Will Pass*, Dar Al Tamarrod, Syria, [n.d]

These three stages give a general picture of the mechanism through which IS controlled Iraq and the Syrian city of Al Raqqa, which it took hold of and turned into its capital in June 2014. IS began to seduce the population under its control by sowing chaos where there was order, establishing new educational, economic, political, judicial and religious institutions, altering their functions or replacing them altogether.

After having established control over the city of Al Raqqa, IS destroyed the Armenian Martyrs' Church and transformed it into an outreach office. This was revealed by British-Palestinian journalist Medyan Dairieh in his documentary *The Islamic State*,[21] which depicts life from inside the city of Al Raqqa after IS control. The documentary aired in August 2014, two months prior to the declaration by an IS spokesman of the creation of the so-called Islamic State of Iraq and Syria.

The documentary devotes considerable time showing the importance IS accords to children following the seizure of the city of Al Raqqa, as well as the subsequent state of children in the wake of the changes implemented by IS members with regards to schooling, indoctrination and their psychological and physical moulding activities. IS created training camps for children of organisation members, children who had relocated with their parents to IS-held regions and children from the regions where IS had established its control, in addition to children abducted from former IS territories after the organisation had withdrawn.

IS turned to other methods as it sought to enhance its allure. One of the tactics it resorted to was luring unemployed youths into recruitment by paying its fighters high salaries and wages, exploiting the financial weakness and soaring unemployment caused by the economic crises in Syria. Another tactic was promoting the personal spoils of war and the enslavement of women,[22] which also proved to be enticing for young men in the West, encouraging them to come and join the ranks of IS. This lure also justifies the presence of foreign and multi-

---

[21] Dairieh. Medyan, *The Islamic State*, [online source], Vice News, available at: https://goo.gl/CDaUTx, published on 14/8/2014, accessed on 20/10/2014

[22] Sabaya: Islamic concept concerning women captured in war. IS distorted its meaning to allow the rape of women captured during IS battles.

national children from France, Australia, Kazakhstan, the UK[23] and other countries. The second section of the paper, which explains the recruitment process, shows the importance of having these children in the ranks of the organisation, and how IS sought to make use of and deploy them in military missions.

Over time, it became clear to IS that such methods had a temporary effect and that new approaches are needed to overcome the difficulties it was facing on the ground. New efforts were made to compensate for its losses, provide an accessible pool of members and ensure its survival. For example, according to a report published on the Monte Carlo Doualiya website, entitled *ISIS Cuts Fighter Wages by Half*[24], in 2016, IS in Al Raqqa was forced to cut its fighters' wages by half. Therefore, in order to overcome such obstacles, the organisation found in children a human resource ripe for the taking. IS began setting up training camps under the name of Cubs of the Caliphate, with the aim of raising a generation indoctrinated by its ideology, in order to ensure its survival and continued success.

Based on the circumstances under which IS emerged and on the mechanisms adopted by the organisation to attract and recruit children, it is clear that the recruitment process is carried out over two key stages: 1) traditional schooling based on a customised IS indoctrination curriculum; and 2) recruitment and ideological, psychological and physical grooming. The paper essentially seeks to unpack these mechanisms and to reveal their effectiveness and impact on children and their way of life, as well as to demonstrate how far IS has gone in inculcating violence and extremism to children recruited in its ranks. As such, the paper will devote the upcoming section to detail the curricula developed and applied by IS, before moving on to discuss the moulding process undergone by children before they are recruited and deployed in combat.

---

[23] Berjawi. Naim, *ISIS exploits 4-year-old British child to execute three Syrians*, [online source], YouTube, available at: https://goo.gl/U5kFTM, published on 12/2/2016, accessed on 20/2/2016

[24] *ISIS cuts fighter wages by half*, [online source], Monte Carlo Doualiya, available at: https://goo.gl/EagKOX, published on 19/1/2016, accessed on 20/1/2016

Second – Schooling in IS-Held Territory

The recruitment and deployment of children to support or participate in armed conflict was practiced by all warring parties in Syria long before IS appeared on the scene. In fact, child soldiers under 14 years of age were first identified in November 2012.[25] They assisted the Free Syrian Army in auxiliary roles. However, the IS recruitment and indoctrination strategy was by far the most intense, in terms of magnitude and method, among all other warring parties—the IS strategy was also the most dangerous, as it gravely violated the rights of children, exploited them in warfare and deprived them of their families.

IS went so far as to display Yazidi and Kurdish children captured in Iraq for sale in public marketplaces. Children between the ages of 1 and 9 were sold for $165,[26] with the price being inversely proportional to the child's age; the younger the child the more impressionable they are and the easier it is to turn them into individuals who carry the IS ideology and seek to realize its expansionist ambitions. The reason why this is so important for IS is that it is currently battling for survival amid a global campaign to wipe it out. IS has created a road for children paved with its ideas, literature and the instruments of its crimes, bombarding them with its propaganda in schools, public spaces and training camps and targeting them in its terrorist operations. Under IS rule, children lost all contact with everything beyond the limits of IS control, due to the policy of obscurantism imposed by the organisation. IS began by changing the curricula, "prompting the illiteracy of over 60,000 students from the governorate of Al Raqqa, and shutting down some 100 schools."[27] IS also replaced the old curricula with specialised ones developed by the leaders of the organisation, with the

---

[25] Motaparthy. Priyanka, "*Maybe we live and maybe we die*," *recruitment and use of children by armed groups in Syria*, Human Rights Watch, US, 2014, p. 6

[26] Yoon. Sangwon, *Islamic State circulates sex slave price list*, [online source], Bloomberg Business, available at: https://goo.gl/7y6LGf, published on 4 August 2015, accessed on 15/3/2016

[27] *Over 60,000 students out of school in Al Raqqa... an entire generation that cannot read or write*, [online source], Raqqa Is Being Slaughtered Silently, available at: http://www.raqqa-sl.com/?p=3511, published on 19/9/2016, accessed on 25/6/2016

aim of restructuring and reshaping the educational approach. The following section will delve deeper into this particular theme.

1 – New Curricula

Ever since it declared a caliphate state in Iraq and Syria in June 2014, IS began to dedicate considerable attention to education, establishing a so-called Diwan (Office) of Education tasked with managing educational services in IS-controlled territories. The Office developed an education policy to guide the various academic stages, which "curtailed schooling from 15 to 9 years."[28] Indeed, "schooling is divided into three stages (elementary, intermediate, and preparatory) and is distributed over nine years. Study in a single year runs over 10 Hijri months divided into two academic terms. The elementary stage consists of five years, followed by two at the intermediate stage, and another two at the preparatory stage, which itself is divided into three tracks: sciences, Islamic sharia and vocational, after which a student graduates and moves on to higher education."[29]

The Diwan of Education issued a statement (Circular № 1) on 8 August 2014 in which it announced a range of modifications to the existing academic process. IS entirely scrapped the subjects of "music, civics, social studies, history, art, physical education, issues in philosophy, sociology and psychology, ancient Islamic religious education and Christian religious education"[30] from the academic curriculum, instead replacing them with other subjects such as: "monotheism, Arabic, including an explanation of Ibn Malik's *Alfiya*, mathematics, physics and chemistry, natural sciences and English."[31]

---

[28]   Al Ayed. Ali, *Education in Al Raqqa under ISIS: Field Study on the Impact of Conflict in Syria*, Democratic Republic Studies Center, 2015, p. 25

[29]   *Islamic State schools kick off first official academic year in Iraq and Syria*, [online source], Dawa Al Haq News Agency, available at: https://dawaalhaq.com/post/3 2054, published on 11/11/2015, accessed on 2/3/2016

[30]   Al Mallah. Ahmad, *Full story of ISIS school curricula under the Islamic caliphate state*, [online source], Huffington Post Arabic, available at: https://goo.gl/IQBmnn, published on 10/12/2015, accessed on 1/1/2016

[31]   Sweid. Rami, *Education in eastern Syria: ISIS destroys future and present of students*, [online source], The New Arab, available at: https://goo.gl/tB5ewG, published on 17/6/2015, accessed on 30/7/2015

IS also released a so-called 'repentance card' to ensure that teachers stuck to the new special teachings and to guide and orient children towards the vision of the new curriculum. IS told male and female teachers in Al Raqqa in February 2015 "to be present at specified centres to declare their repentance from the principles and ideas of the Socialist Arab Baath Party."[32] IS considered these principles to be a form of polytheism that promoted worldly matters at the expense of religious ones. Each teacher had to carry the card after filling and signing it, risking punishment if they failed to do so.

The text of the repentance card itself serves as evidence on the intimidation tactics adopted by IS in its control and supervision of teachers. Through this method, IS sought to assert full control over the education sector and to recruit teachers as an indirect yet active means to achieve its aims. The text of the repentance card reads: "I, the undersigned, hereby repent before Allah for what I have done (…) I hereby declare my innocence of the false nationalist, patriotic and Baathist curricula, and my innocence of complying with man-made laws and the worship of idols. I voluntarily submit to and accept the rule of Allah Almighty. I pledge not to disobey what is good, and not to fight or abet fighting against Muslims, either in words or deeds. I shall abide by Allah's prohibitions and never overstep His restrictions. Should I deviate or change, I shall be exposed to the judgment of Allah Almighty."[33] Thus, IS surrounds and cultivates children as soon as the stage of early childhood, by controlling their sources of immediate knowledge and by orienting their budding awareness towards certain aspects favourable to the IS worldview.

IS supports these measures with more radical steps to bolster its position and its ability to brainwash children through the exclusive teaching of its curricula. The process of teaching IS ideology was first shaped through a set of instructions released by the organisation. The instructions consisted of several points, including those published by IS Diwan of Education officer Dhul Qarnayn.[34] "The instructions prescribed removing the phrase Syrian Arab Republic wherever it ap-

---

[32] Al Ayed. Ali, *Education in Al Raqqa under ISIS*, op. cit., p. 15

[33] Al Ayed. Ali, *Education in Al Raqqa under ISIS*, ibid., p. 60

[34] German national of Egyptian descent, he is the chief supervisor of the committee developing curricula for the organisation.

peared, and replacing it with Islamic State."[35] Instructions further stipulated "cancelling the Syrian national anthem wherever it appeared, refraining from teaching the concepts of patriotism and nationalism and replacing them with notions about Islam and its community, and replacing the terms 'nation, their nation, Syria or my nation' wherever they appeared by 'the Islamic State, their Islamic State, land of Muslims or wilaya of the Levant'." The statement featured "removing all examples, in mathematics, suggesting usury or usurious interests, democracy or elections, removing everything, in sciences, related to Darwin's theory, natural evolution or creation out of nothing, and ascribing all creation to Allah Almighty."[36] IS made these instructions binding; all incompliance incurred punishment and accountability.

2 – Inculcating IS Ideology and Building the Jihadi Identity

The modification of school curricula to match the ideology of IS teachings shows the importance of education and schooling as a tool for creating a conceptual body, encompassing the vocabulary and concepts related to teaching, society and social relationships from the organisation's perspective. Anyone who spoke against these concepts would be discredited and punished. This conceptual body or institutions inevitably distinguishes children in IS areas from other children of the same age elsewhere. Children thus become responsible for and are tasked with spreading what they have learned to others in their society, especially after receiving religious instruction through mosque sessions focused on transmitting radical and extremist religious thought to the minds of children. For example, "the writings of Muhammad bin Abdul Wahhab, such as his books *Kitab Al Tawhid* (Book of the Unity of God), *Kashf Al Shubuhat* (Clarification of Doubts), and *Nawaqid Al Islam* (Nullifiers of Islam), are distributed in IS-controlled regions in Iraq and

---

[35] *Over 60,000 students out of school in Al Raqqa… an entire generation that cannot read and write*, op. cit.

[36] *Dhul Qarnayn issues statement specifying list of modifications to school curricula in Islamic State*, [online source], Aks Alser, available at: https://goo.gl/uuhsPj, published on 29/8/2014, accessed on 1/3/2016

Syria, displaying the seal and black and white motto of IS. The books are taught and explained in special religious sessions."[37]

All of these writings depict 'others' as apostates and teach societies to reject them. The readers of these books cannot be expected to discuss the material with children, given the extremely complex vocabulary and ideas on apostasy and other complex religious matters. Such writings serve to create a limited religious reference or knowledge for children, as well as a background of concepts consisting of IS words and jargon far removed from common or civil terminology. As a result, children acquire a glossary of terms like: Islamic *wilaya*, Islamic State, apostasy, infidels, death, slaughter, caliph, land of apostasy, land of Muslims, *jihadi*, etc.

In addition such writings, IS aims to further spread its extremist teachings containing much incitement to kill others. Literature by researchers in the field of Islamic and radical groups are chock-full of the principles of IS members and the teachings repeated among children during instruction or in training camps. These consist of fifteen principles declared by the former head of the organisation in Iraq, Abu Omar Al Baghdadi, including: "We deem jihad in the name of Allah an appointed duty, since the fall of Al Andalus, to liberate the land of Muslims. He is with every righteous person and wicked sinner, and the worst sin after apostasy is to prohibit jihad in the name of Allah at the time appointed by Him. Indeed, Ibn Hazm said, 'There is no greater sin after apostasy than prohibiting jihad against the apostates.'"[38] The aim is for IS to achieve what it calls 'the bond and belonging', or to ensure the critical importance of belonging to IS—in words, in deeds and in thought—by instilling in children the key concepts of the organisation. Loyalty to IS is guaranteed insofar as a child continues to be surrounded by and to live by these concepts and words. This is an indication of the centrality of targeting children to ensure the survival of the fighting power of IS.

---

[37]   Ibrahim. Fuad, *ISIS from Al Najdi to Al Baghdadi*, op. cit. p. 128

[38]   These principles have appeared in several resources, although not in any particular order. Sources: *ISIS from Al Najdi to Al Baghdadi; The real Islamic State; ISIS between fact and fiction; ISIS in Iraq and Syria in the balance of Sunna and Islam.*

This tie and sense of belonging are evident in the video *My Father Told Me*,[39] produced by IS's propaganda department. It tells the story of a group of children aged between 9 and 12, in training camps, as they carry out the wishes of their fathers to continue to fight. Children are inevitably the most sensitive to social and communal ties and any sense of belonging to the group. It is for this reason that IS members entice the largest possible number of children, approaching them through parties and events and attracting them through the distribution of presents.

Unifying ideas, vocabulary, images, dress code and memories for children creates a special identity for them, and thus it becomes easier to manipulate their interactions and/or reactions to the various situations they face, in order to ensure their compliance with the worldview of the organisation. This was the reason why IS lured children into cub camps that, as will be shown in the following section, aim to produce a generation that carries the very traits and ideas of IS members. IS does not deploy efforts that do not serve its aims, i.e. pandering to and enticing children until they are in its clutches, after which it can begin to indoctrinate them with radical principles.

Although the term "Ashbal" (cubs) signifies for IS "those under 16 who have been trained in IS camps and were relied on in the past for the execution of prisoners and suicide missions, since they did not raise the suspicion of soldiers when crossing checkpoints, they have recently been used in battles as a result of IS's massive loss of trained members."[40] Filmed reports and videos published by IS and/or its partisans on propaganda websites illustrated the recruitment of three, four, five, nine or ten-year-olds who were assigned all types of military missions and currently obey orders without objection. The documentary *He Made Me Alive with His Blood*,[41] produced by IS, shows children aged three who were recruited and trained to kill. It also tells the stories of some of its cub members who preferred the life of the organisation over living with their own families.

---

[39] Trailer is available at: https://goo.gl/KfJYSU, accessed on 21/8/2016

[40] Kano. Sadr Al Din, *Soon, ISIS to recruit child soldiers*, [online source], ARANEWS, available at: https://goo.gl/MVbZmA, published on 19/8/2016, accessed on 21/8/2016

[41] Documentary available at: https://goo.gl/kGXi7j, accessed on 21/8/2016

Third – Recruitment in IS-Held Territory– Cub Camps

The following section will answer the core question of the paper, which is: how successful has IS been in grooming a generation that is committed to its ideology and carries its culture? What are the adverse impacts that may arise from the emergence of such a generation? Are we dealing with a transient recruitment that is part and parcel of any armed conflict, whose victims just happen to be children, and which inevitably ends when wars and conflicts draw to a close?

The strategies analysed and illustrated in the section on education as being key to indoctrinate and acclimatise children to IS discourse and culture have paved the way for recruitment, which typically took place post-schooling. At times, children were recruited without being schooled at first, because the cost of war has forced the organisation to accelerate the pace of recruitment and even to overlook indoctrination through schooling.

However, in both cases, recruiting children follows a defined course, which this paper will explain in the following section. This course begins with reaching out to and attracting children, before moving on to mental and physical training, and culminating in a groomed generation.

1 – Reaching Out to Children and Initiating Child Selection

The educational process and its supportive role in attracting and recruiting children continue to hinge solely on those children who are enrolled in schools. In order to attract the largest number of youths, IS organises recreational and community activities in public squares in areas under its control. These activities are often contests that focus on questions concerned with the memorisation of the Quran and the Traditions (Hadith) of Prophet Muhammad. Awards and prizes are given to the winners, in an attempt by IS to establish trust with children and build a kind of friendship with them.

An incident that shows how this strategy was utilised and that casts light on how children are enticed and lured by IS members is the campaign entitled *Your Rockets Will Not Silence the Smiles of Children*,[42] organised in October 2014 in Al Raqqa, Syria. After the anti-ISIS International Coalition began bombing the Syrian city of Al Raqqa in September 2014, hitting children in the strikes, IS members visited hospitals and checked on injured children, bringing them presents, toys, flowers and prizes that they distributed during their visits.

What is really evident in such campaigns is that IS fighters are portrayed as smiling and compassionate, contrary to the faces of fighters shown in IS videos on military operations and other activities. IS is well aware that angry, scowling faces do not lure and entice children. However, to balance out such generosity and ease (presents and prizes), children are routinely encouraged to watch public executions. Children are shown filmed executions and are sometimes even brought to attend them in person. In IS promotional videos, you can see children pushing through the crowds of adults for a courtside view of the event, be it a beheading or a crucifixion.

This outreach to children is not limited to IS-controlled regions. In fact, children are also targeted by IS beyond its borders, through the release of video games developed on behalf of the organisation. IS has released its own version of Grand Theft Auto[43], which is a hugely popular game among children over the world. The IS game, however, begins with *Allah Akbar* chants, and the player is given a wide array of choices for fighting (assassination, sniping, rigging explosives, raiding headquarters, etc.). The soundtrack of the game is the famous IS anthem *Salil Al Sawarem* (Clash of Swords).

This is one factor that might explain the presence of children from different nationalities, both Arab and Western, within IS ranks. This is ascribed to the fact that the organisation in Syria includes foreign and non-Arab members, a fact that has been confirmed by several IS releases, such as *He Made Me Alive with His Blood*, and a report titled *ISIS*

---

[42] *New IS release: Your rockets will not silence the smiles of children*, [online source], YouTube, available at: https://goo.gl/KbJ7NZ, published on 15/10/2015, accessed on 8/3/2016

[43] 24 News 2, *How does ISIS recruit children through video games?* [online source], YouTube, available at: https://goo.gl/2td5lY, published on 17/9/2015, accessed on 5/3/2016

Training Children of Foreign Fighters to Become 'Next Generation' of Terrorists,[44] which revealed some 50 British children training and fighting with IS.

The process of luring children is merely the first of a series of other steps. Education and recreational activities for children and adolescents are followed by the selection of specific and individual children for relocation to special camps, away from schools and public squares. Those who are selected are given priority by IS to go into the Cubs of the Caliphate camps.[45]

A special breed of children are trained in these camps, characterised by gruelling physical activity. Focused study is reserved for Islamic doctrine and history from the perspective of IS. Children graduate from the course with the title of "cub" and are assigned missions. "Selected children fall under five categories: children born to foreign or immigrant fighters, those born to local fighters, those who were abandoned and found their way to IS orphanage, those who were forcefully taken from their parents and those who voluntarily joined the organisation."[46]

Once the children are selected, they are taken to the dedicated camp. They are first enrolled in a 45-day sharia course,[47] which consists of memorising the Quran and hadiths on killing and apostasy. "Afterwards, children are subjected to a military course that lasts for three months. Children train with live ammunition inside what is known as the "house of killing," an indoor shooting range used to train conscripts, using live rounds, in infiltration and taking over a residential

---

[44] Dearden. Lizzie, *ISIS training children of foreign fighters to become 'next generation' of terrorists*, [online source], Independent, available at: https://goo.gl/6I83Pm, published on 29/7/2016, accessed on 2/8/2016

[45] It is worth mentioning that IS has several known camps for training children, including: 1) Al Zarqawi Camp; 2) Osama bin Laden Camp; 3) Sharia cub camps for children under 16; 4) Sharkarak Camp; 5) Pioneers Camp.

[46] Abdul Majid. Ahmad, *ISIS methods of persuasion in recruiting members: A scientific approach*, Al Baheth Al Ilmi Magazine, 2016

[47] For more on child trainings and mechanisms, refer to the videos:
Abas. Hsham, *IS children's training camp*, [online source], YouTube, available at: https://goo.gl/tsKfN0, published on 22/6/2015, accessed on 6/3/2016
Karbala Agency News (KAN), *ISIS children trained in slaughter and killing*, [online source], YouTube, available at: https://goo.gl/VPqf9B, published on 1/10/2014, accessed on 6/3/2016

building. Children also learn how to get to and invade the building before moving from room to room. They learn how to subdue others and use them as hostages. Children are trained in sniping and how to ambush a moving vehicle. IS then exposes children to the violent scenes it practices, and encourages them to practice and participate in them."[48]

Other videos published by IS show children carrying severed heads and participating in beheadings themselves. A number of IS fighters published photos of their sons helping them decapitate others. For example, Khaled Sharrouf, an Australian IS fighter of Lebanese descent, posted a photo of his 7-year-old son holding the severed head of a Syrian opposition fighter. "A short video shows another child carrying the head of the General Sharia Judge of Suqour Al Sham Brigade (Falcons of the Levant), Abu Abdul Samih, after the invasion of the town of Akhtrin on 14 August 2014."[49]

Trainings for beheadings know no age limits. IS published a video in which a child beheads his doll—he is barely three years old.[50] Dressed like IS members, the child holds a large knife in his hand. He then beheads his doll, yelling *Allah Akbar*. The child's method in beheading the doll is evidence of his intense training; the way the child moves, dresses and brandishes the knife are reminiscent of the famous IS decapitator "Jihadi John" who was killed in an Alliance strike in 2015.

2 – Mental and Physical Training and Distribution of Military Roles

When children graduate from cub camps, military missions are assigned to each child/cub. They are each given an alias after leaving the course at the camp. These missions are carried out either individually

---

[48] *Cubs of the Caliphate... Role of children inside ISIS*, [online source], Rawabet Center for Research and Strategic Studies, available at: https://goo.gl/zCDzZC, published on 24/7/2015, accessed on 30/7/2017

[49] *ISIS kills childhood: Special report on ISIS violations against children in Syria*, [online source], Syrian Human Rights Committee, available at: http://www.shrc.org/?p=19219, published on 16/8/2014, accessed on 5/3/2016

[50] Williams. Evan, *ISIS' children: Soldiers trained to kill and die*, [online source], Channel 4 News, available at: https://goo.gl/LKFKuE, published on 1/10/2015, accessed on 11/5/2015

or collectively by a group. Examples of such missions are: execution by gunfire,[51] decapitations (for example, a child under 10 years of age beheaded a pilot serving with the Syrian army who had been captured by IS in a battle[52]) or helping supply ammunition during battle. Recruited children are additionally used in IS ranks as spies, since the perception of children as young and innocent can be exploited to discover dissent and opposition to IS rule among the local population. Finally, they can be sent on suicide missions. One of the implementers of the suicide mission at IS-captured Al Tabqa military airbase was a 12-year-old child.

At times, the organisation seeks to promote, through its videos and publications, that children's participation in IS activities is done with the parents' blessings. In this context, IS published a video entitled *My Son Preceded Me*[53] on 21 February 2016. The video tells the story of a father who urged his son to detonate an explosive device after registering his name for a martyrdom operation in IS lists. The child agreed to his father's request and promised to meet him again in paradise. The boy was fifteen years of age, nicknamed Abu Ammara Al Omari, and he killed himself in a car bomb in rural Aleppo. In the video, the boy explained that he was originally from the Al Sakhour district in the city of Aleppo. He had migrated to the IS-held town of Qabasin in north-eastern rural Aleppo with his family and joined IS when he was fourteen. The child, Abu Ammara, was stationed on IS frontlines in northern rural Aleppo until his father put his name down for a martyrdom operation. The video published showed the child on Dabiq hill, in the countryside of Aleppo, speaking to an IS member. The video also showed the child's father approving of his sons words and actions, helping him into the car and teaching him how to drive it. The final

---

[51] Sky News Arabia, *ISIS child kills Palestinian on the charge of spying for Israel*, [online source], YouTube, available at: https://goo.gl/0Yhaxm, published on 11/3/2015, accessed on 10/3/2016

[52] Alkout Taqareer, *Child recruited by ISIS beheads Syrian pilot*, [online source], YouTube, available at: https://goo.gl/XRZFsN, published on 18/7/2015, accessed on 10/3/2016

[53] The video was removed from the internet due to its bloody and violent content after it was published on 21/2/2016. Some images from the video before it was deleted can be found at: https://goo.gl/bG3sHp, accessed on 3/3/2016

scene is this child fighter blowing himself up in a car bomb in rural Aleppo.

One can say that the current generation of children and adolescents being groomed by IS is much more dangerous, given their training and indoctrination, than the previous generations who were raised under similar circumstances of extremism and radical thought. Their danger lies in the fact that they were raised on and imbued with caliphate teachings and vocabulary since their birth. This generation has not heard of or seen other regimes, be they dictatorships, secular, leftist or moderate religious.

This has contributed to children living in IS areas having a distinctive character from other children in regions not under IS control. This paper will present a profile of this character, which it has termed the "jihadi character", and how it was utilised by the organisation to maximize public and media attention. The presentation will attempt to deduce the perfect prototype that IS strives to generate for recruiting and attracting children. IS is well aware of the value and importance of children who can be deployed, once they have been indoctrinated and militarised, to ensure sustained sabotage, killing, sexual violations and ongoing oppression and activities under the IS banner. It is also interesting to note that these children amplify in number and use when the organisation sustains successive defeats.

3 – The Jihadi Character

Children who are schooled and raised in IS camps have a distinctive character that sets them apart from other children in terms of dress, background knowledge, perception, speech, intonation, the use of arms and public speaking. The character of these children is moulded by intense training and courses at the hands of IS leaders.

The character of a jihadi child takes on two aspects that IS videos and reports indicate. The first is when a single child is filmed as the star of a video published by the organisation, and the second is when a group of children perform as an ensemble. The celebrity status or the starring role here is not exclusive to any one child but rather shared by a group of children, e.g. the aforementioned release *He Made Me Alive with His Blood*. These characters are diverse; they are oratory characters whose role consists of public speaking and performing moving anthems for rallying children and adolescents. Such speeches and anthems abound online: in one video, for instance, a child delivers a sermon at a mosque during Ramadan before a large crowd, making threats to the White House and the US in his address[54]. But the child character that stands out the most amid the ranks of the organisation is the one in which all the traits of a gifted child converge, employed by IS members to create a typical jihadi child. These traits comprise: physical beauty, melodious voice, catchy name, special training for good performance in combat, and full memorisation of the Quran and hadiths.

These traits were united in the "Cub of Al Baghdadi[55]", the first Emirati child whose death with his father was announced by IS on 7 October 2014. The child was Muhammad Al Absi Abu Obeida, dubbed "The Cub of Al Baghdadi", after the Caliph Abu Bakr Al Baghdadi. IS poets composed poems mourning, praising, and eulogising this child after his death. Short videos featuring photos of him in various poses, armed to the teeth and in full gear, were shown. The videos were accompanied by songs performed by the child himself in honour of the caliph.

These characters, and the propaganda they exemplify with the use of modern technology, have significance and impact as poster children or super-boys, which IS promotes in their programmes targeting children. "The Cub of Al Baghdadi", and other children like him, have the same influence as fictional TV or story characters in children's programmes. The charisma of a child like "The Cub of Al Baghdadi" is the first factor in attracting other children: his exotic and exciting dress, the large firearms he wields despite his minute size, the songs he performs, not to mention the amount of followers he enjoys on social media.

---

[54] *Small speech by a caliphate cub*, [online source], YouTube, available at: https://goo.gl/eRi65b, published on 28/6/2015, accessed on 12/2/2016

[55] Hall. John, *Our youngest martyr: ISIS boasts a jihadi fighter aged just TEN was killed as he went into battle with his father in Syria*, [online source], Mail Online, available at: https://goo.gl/gn9RNJ, published on 9/10/2014, accessed on 1/12/2014

Conclusion

This paper has attempted to present the mechanism of child recruitment within IS ranks, as well as to illuminate the different aspects and the historical context of such programmes. The study has touched on the pre-recruitment stage, consisting of radical changes to the school system/curriculum, and the opening of schools with traditional educational missions that were in fact nothing but institutions teaching children the arts of combat, imbuing them with IS doctrine and thought. This is in addition to child outreach activities by way of games, contests and prizes. The study also addressed the roles performed by children, sometimes through coercion and/or trickery, which resulted in the death of hundreds of them. The children of Syria and Iraq have become a human resource for the organisation's future, carrying its ideology and passing on its thought to upcoming generations.

The paper has also exposed how IS has benefited from children, how it targets them and how it designs strategies to control them. As indicated throughout the research, the purpose of such control and recruitment of children is not coincidental. The chief aim of targeting children is to implant the thought and doctrine of IS in their hearts and minds. Children's minds are like a sponge, absorbing the ideas, actions and behaviours they are exposed to. Through such indoctrination strategies, IS ensures that its ideas are protected and remain resilient for a long time to come. Ideas grow and develop along with IS itself, meaning that IS doctrine will endure for generations and generations to come.

IS threatens to produce and export a new generation that is, in its words, more vigilant and protective of Islam than the current one. This can be confirmed by the figures and statistics presented in the study about children recruited by IS, as well as by other figures that were not included due to the difficulty of obtaining required documentation. This does not include schools, universities and institutes closed by IS, its restrictions on schooling and the banning of all types of entertainment and recreation for children. Children recruited by IS become desensitised to scenes of violence; flogging, crucifixion and stoning, bandying severed heads, participating in slaughter and killing and inciting such violence through speeches and sermons. All these actions and situations that children are exposed to become part of their memory, their consciousness, and create a blueprint for their future. As a result of children being raised on these principles, criminal acts becomes normal, perhaps even welcome, and are not met with any rejection or questioning.

Here lies the difference between IS and other armed groups operating in Syria, whether regime- or opposition-affiliated, which have training and instruction camps for children under 18 and deploy children to the battlefield: IS gives far greater attention to children, and it does not only school and recruit them for a temporary state of conduct and then allow them to return to their normal lives. What children under IS rule learn is an entire approach and worldview, a mind-set or way of life that they practice their whole life through, both in war and peace. The core belief of this mind-set is disagreement with anyone who had different view, and aiming to win over disagreeing opinions by all means until they align with their own. For other organisations, the primary reason for recruiting youths is a shortage of fighters and a need for more people to carry weapons in big battles. Only IS has been observed to send children as suicide bombers against military positions in cars rigged with explosives, or to use a child to verbally threaten the White House and apostates with slaughter and punishment on IS websites.

Studying this topic was no easy task: the researcher faced several obstacles, among which the near impossibility of obtaining documented, detailed information about the organisation, especially with regards to its educational systems and recruitment mechanisms. This is due firstly to the immediacy of these practices, and secondly to the media war against IS, which prompts internet users worldwide to report websites that post information about or promote the organisation in order to shut them down. This has clearly made information gathering and documentation more difficult. It is also worth noting that the researcher was keen on ensuring the largest degree of accuracy by methodically documenting information and specifying all the references and sources used in the research.

In the final analysis, one might pose the following question: what is the difference between showing a child who was raised in IS camps scenes of beheading or crucifixion, and showing the same scenes to a child who has never been exposed to such violence? This question does not seek to find a ready and imagined answer that lists the differences between the two scenarios, as much as it invokes the issue of humanity, and how much these children have been deprived of it. Their basic human rights and humanity have been violated and their thoughts poisoned by toxic IS ideas, which are lethal to any society. Children, as far as IS is concerned, are seeds that can be planted in a fertile soil to ensure a blooming future that recreates the glories of the organisation in the long term.

Finally, the purpose of raising the subject of child recruitment and the mass violations of children's rights is to draw further attention to the magnitude of the suffering experienced by children in Syria and Iraq as a result of IS practices. By highlighting the impacts and consequences of child recruitment, this paper hopes to act as a resource for international and human and children's rights organisations. Furthermore, the paper's findings might also serve as reference material on the phenomenon for local relief associations operating in Syria when planning their interventions, thus optimising their understanding of what children's lives were like under IS. It is with this knowledge that actors working to support children in Syria and Iraq can design better methods for dealing with children who were psychologically scarred by IS activity and practices against their childhood.

Appendix I: Figures and Statistics, Number of Recruited Children and Number of Child Fatalities among Recruits

- In February 2016, IS graduated the first cohort of child fighters in its ranks. At least 175 child fighters graduated from this group. They were sent to the battlefronts in rural Al Raqqa. In January 2016, IS graduated a class of some 450 members, including approximately 100 children who were enrolled in "Cubs of the Caliphate" camps, originally from the governorates of Homs, Aleppo and Al Raqqa. The ceremony was attended by several IS military commanders, both Syrian and foreign, and was held once the trainees had completed their military training, which the organisation had shortened from two months to just one.[56]

- On 19 February 2016, The Independent newspaper published a news story entitled *Isis Is Using Far More Child Soldiers than the World Realized*,[57] which contained a timeline on the emergence of IS in more than 40 pictures, between 2000 and 2015, with information explaining each picture and its significance. The year 2000 was chosen as the date for the emergence of the organisation, given that Abu Musab Al Zarqawi is considered to be the spiritual father of IS.

- A study developed by the Firil Center for Studies, Berlin, stated that the largest gathering of foreign fighters in history occurred in Syria, consisting of 360,000 foreign fighters, among whom were 3,200 Jordanians and 24,500 Saudis, with the largest portion being part of IS, between April 2011 and January 2016—which is the period covered in the study.[58] Today, in 2017, there are only 90,000 foreign fighters left.

---

[56] *News, IS graduates 450 fighters among whom approximately 100 children from Cubs of Caliphate camp from Aleppo and Al Raqqa*, [online source], The Syrian Observatory for Human Rights, available at: https://goo.gl/Z2IBmg, published on 9/1/2016, accessed on 1/3/2016

[57] Article available at https://goo.gl/fBYyju, accessed on 1/3/2016

[58] Shaheen. M Jameel, *More than 360 foreign fighters have fought the Syrian Army*, [online source], Firil Center for Studies, Berlin, available at: http://firil.net/?p=2428, published on 19/2/2016, accessed on 28/2/2016

Appendix II: Selected International Condemnations and Statements Issued on Child Recruitment

- In July 2013, the UNHCR released a report titled *From Slow Boil to Breaking Point*,[59] presenting its own assessment of the state of Syrian refugees, which revealed that the agency considered child recruitment by armed groups a key protection issue.
- In March 2013, Save the Children,[60] an international NGO advocating children's rights, announced, in a report titled *Two Million Syrian Children Caught in Crossfire of Conflict Entering its Third Year*, the growing number of children "who are exposed to direct risks as they are being recruited by armed forces and groups."[61]
- On 13 February 2015, UNICEF issued a detailed statement on the International Day against the Use of Child Soldiers, reiterating the danger of children being involved in the war in Syria and the critical need to take action to protect them.[62]
- The International Conference on Reducing Child Recruitment was held on 15 June 2015 in Baghdad. The conference provided recommendations to reduce recruitment and warned that ISIS had opened four camps in Nineveh to recruit nearly 1,000 children under 18 years of age.

---

[59] Crisp. Jeff, *From slow boil to breaking point*, [pdf], UNHCR report, published on 10/7/2013

[60] For the official NGO website please visit: https://goo.gl/9Xxiu8

[61] *Two million Syrian children caught in crossfire of conflict entering its third year, Save the Children warns*, [online source], Save the Children, available at: https://goo.gl/Su6h2Y, published on 13/3/2013, accessed on 10/11/2015

[62] Al Dimashqi. Youmna, *Syrian children... On the international day against the use of child soldiers*, [online source], Arabi 21, available at: https://goo.gl/gWS7UP, published on 15/2/2015, accessed on 10/2/2016

Appendix III: Key Dates in IS Timeline

- On 9 April 2013, Al Baghdadi announced the disbanding of the Nusra Front and its integration into the Islamic State of Iraq (ISI), under the new name of the Islamic State of Iraq and Syria (ISIS).[63] Nusra refused this merger and pledged allegiance to Ayman Al Zawahiri.

- On 9 June 2013, Ayman Al Zawahiri asked that Abu Bakr Al Baghdadi disband ISIS and called for separating the areas of Nusra and ISIS operations, so as to have ISIS operate only in Iraq while Nusra focuses its activity in Syria under the command of Abu Mohammad Al Julani. Abu Bakr Al Baghdadi refused Al Zawahiri's request.[64]

- In September 2013, IS killed the leader of Ahrar Al Sham Brigade, Abu Obeida, and captured the city of Azaz in rural Aleppo from the Free Syrian Army. Azaz was a strategic city for IS, given its proximity to the Turkish border and its potential for being used as a crossing point for foreign fighters and for the delivery of financial and military assistance across the border.

- In February, the dispute between IS and the former Nusra Front turned into open fighting, during which Nusra stood alongside the Free Syrian Army brigades in a bid to expel IS from the governorate of Deir Al Zor. However, IS killed, in a suicide operation, one commander and six members of the Ahrar Al Sham movement, as well as a tribal sheikh from the Awakening forces and several of his followers in the Iraqi city of Haditha.[65]

- In June, IS scored successive victories, seizing control of the governorate of Mosul where two brigades of the Iraqi army had surrendered their weapons. Their number was estimated at 30,000 troops. Moreover, half a million residents fled from Mosul, including 400 families from the Christian minority. IS executed 670 Shiite prisoners who had been detained in Badosh Prison, Mosul. IS also captured most of the governorates of Ni-

[63] Manna. Haytham, *The ISIS Caliphate*, The Scandinavian Institute for Human Rights (SIHR), Geneva, 2014, p. 82

[64] Fuad. Ibrahim, *ISIS from Al Najdi to Al Baghdadi*, op. cit. p. 124

[65] Atwan. Abdel Bari, *The Islamic State*, op. cit., p. 36

neveh and Tikrit, and several towns in the governorate of Sala-din. The organisation besieged the Yazidis in Amerli, resulting in the death of numerous individuals. IS abducted thousands of Yazidi women, while some 50,000 Yazidis fled to the mountains of Sinjar.[66]

- On 19 June, IS tightened its hold in Iraq on the chemical weap-ons facility in Muthana, the city of Tal Afar and its strategic air-base.[67] In Syria, it captured Al Omar oil field from the Nusra Front and Al Shaer gas field in Homs.[68]

- On 29 June, IS spokesman Abu Mohammad Al Adnani declared the establishment of a caliphate state and pledged allegiance to Abu Bakr Al Baghdadi as caliph of all Muslims.

- On 15 August, the Security Council issued Resolution 2170, which stated that "the Security Council expressed concern that terrorist foreign fighters are joining the ranks of ISIS and Nusra Front (...) The two organisations constitute a threat to interna-tional peace; therefore, Chapter VII of the UN Charter must be applied."[69]

- In late August, NATO member states created an international al-liance to strike the organisation. The alliance began bombing IS positions on 19 September 2014.

- In 2015, IS started losing numerous positions and haemorrhag-ing fighters as its top leaders were being targeted. 2015 was admittedly a year of defeats for the organisation. US Secretary of State John Kerry stated, on the side-lines of the World Eco-nomic Forum in Davos, Switzerland: "We are costing ISIS big losses today. It has lost 40% of the territories it held in Iraq, be-tween 20–30% in total. I believe that the organisation will be greatly weakened in Iraq and Syria by the end of 2016."[70] An-other indicator of the decline of IS are media reports stating that the organisation was suffering from a shortage in the num-ber of its troops following the hits it had sustained. This primari-ly forced it, for the first time ever, to call for mobilisation, "allow-

---

[66] Atwan. Abdel Bari, *The Islamic State*, ibid., p. 38

[67] Atwan. Abdel Bari, *The Islamic State*, ibid., p. 37

[68] Atwan. Abdel Bari, *The Islamic State*, ibid., p. 38

[69] Manna. Haytham, *The ISIS Caliphate*, op. cit., p. 83

[70] *Death of 22,000 ISIS members since summer 2014*, [online source], Al Arabiya, available at: https://goo.gl/BB0ryI, published on 22/1/2016, accessed on 25/4/2017

ing individuals wishing to fight alongside the organisation to join without pledging allegiance to the Islamic State and caliph (...) Sources believe that such an extraordinary measure was likely due to the shortage of organisation members, and a bid to reinforce its forces in the city."[71] Children, the majority of whom under sixteen, were not exempt from such mobilisation and were used in the Kobani or Ayn Al Arab battle. "The bodies of 30 children under 18 were delivered to the city of Al Raqqa. Those children, once they had completed the Sharia course, were immediately sent to a one-month combat course (...) Of the suicide operations carried out in Kobani, one had been performed by a child named Bassel Humeira from the city of Al Raqqa who had not reached the age of 18."[72]

- In 2016, IS was plagued by massive losses in the number of its fighters, according to statements by British and US officials. However, the two camps continued to disagree on the accurate figures of IS members who had been killed since the start of alliance strikes. While UK Secretary of State for Defence Michael Fallon put the number at 25,000 members, a US official gave another figure, which was 50,000.[73] The figures, however, remain estimates, given the difficulty of access and documentation in IS territory, and the punishment of any non-member who tries to do so.

---

[71]   *Without pledging allegiance to the caliph... IS enlists dozens to fight in its ranks in Deir ez-Zor*, [online source], The Syrian Observatory for Human Rights, available at: https://goo.gl/d9rVw5, published on 31/1/2016, accessed on 25/4/2017

[72]   Qasem. Roshan, *ISIS teaches children "terrorism" at its military schools*, [online source], Majalla, available at: https://goo.gl/PNdqb7, published on 16/10/2014, accessed on 1/3/2016

[73]   Browne. Ryan, *UK puts number of ISIS fighters killed at half US figure*, [online source], CNN Politics, available at: https://goo.gl/HVgJo0, published on 16/12/2016, accessed on 25/12/2016

Sources and References

Books

Amro. Abu Sefian; Al Kradsi. Sadat; Al Noubi. Abu Ziad Muhammad Yaqoub, *The Real Islamic State...ISIS: Documented Sayings of Group Emirs and Leaders*, [n.p.], [n.d.]

Abu Bakr. Naji, *Management of Savagery: The Most Critical Stage through which the Islamic Nation Will Pass*, Dar Al Tamarrod, Syria, [n.d.]

Al Ayed. Ali, *Education in Al Raqqa under ISIS: Field Study on the Impact of Conflict in Syria*, Democratic Republic Studies Center, 2015

Atwan. Abdel Bari, *The Islamic State: The Roots, the Savagery and the Future*, Dar al Saqi, Beirut, 2015

Ibrahim. Fuad, *ISIS from Al Najdi to Al-Baghdadi: Nostalgia for the Caliphate*, Awal Centre for Studies and Documentation, Beirut, 2015

Manna. Haytham, *The ISIS Caliphate*, The Scandinavian Institute for Human Rights (SIHR), Geneva, 2014

Motaparthy. Priyanka, *"Maybe We Live and Maybe We Die," Recruitment and Use of Children by Armed Groups in Syria*, Human Rights Watch, US, 2014

Articles

Abu Zeid. Adnan, *Birds of Paradise: Project of rape and explosive belts*, [online source], Iraqi Women's League – IWL, available at: https://goo.gl/TI8EsF, published on 30/5/2009, accessed on 3/3/2016

Al Mallah. Ahmad, *Full story of ISIS school curricula under the Islamic caliphate state*, [online source], Huffington Post Arabic, available at: https://goo.gl/IQBmnn, published on 10/12/2015, accessed on 1/1/2016

Cubs of the Caliphate... Role of children inside ISIS, [online source], Rawabet Center for Research and Strategic Studies, available at: https://goo.gl/zCDzZC, published on 24/7/2015, accessed on 30/7/2017

Death of 22,000 ISIS members since summer 2014, [online source], Al Arabiya, available at: https://goo.gl/BB0ryl, published on 22/1/2016, accessed on 25/4/2017

Details of the full operation: How children are recruited into ISIS ranks, [online source], Orient Net, available at: https://goo.gl/MlteVp, published on 25/7/2015, accessed on 1/3/2016

Dhul Qarnayn issues statement specifying list of modifications to school curricula in Islamic State, [online source], Aks Alser, available at: https://goo.gl/uuhsPj, published on 29/8/2014, accessed on 1/3/2016

ISIS cuts fighter wages by half, [online source], Monte Carlo Doualiya, available at: https://goo.gl/EagKOX, published on 19/1/2016, accessed on 20/1/2016

ISIS-held regions in Iraq and Syria [online source], Al Arabiya, available at: https://goo.gl/BlBLum, published on 3/3/2015, accessed on 1/4/2015

ISIS kills childhood: Special report on ISIS violations against children in Syria, [online source], Syrian Human Rights Committee, available at: http://www.shrc.org/?p=19219, published on 16/8/2014, accessed on 5/3/2016

Islamic State schools kick off first official academic year in Iraq and Syria, [online source], Dawa Al Haq News Agency, available at: https://dawaalhaq.com/post/32054, published on 11/11/2015, accessed on 2/3/2016

Iraq: Children between harsh present and unknown future, [online source], Child Rights International Network (CRIN) website, available at https://goo.gl/ZwUfKg, published on 28/9/2008, accessed on 10/1/2016

Kano. Sadr Al Din, *Soon, ISIS to recruit child soldiers*, [online source], ARANEWS, available at: https://goo.gl/MVbZmA, published on 19/8/2016, accessed on 21/8/2016

News, IS graduates 450 fighters among whom approximately 100 children from Cubs of Caliphate camp from Aleppo and Al Raqqa, [online source], The Syrian Observatory for Human Rights, available at: https://goo.gl/Z2lBmg, published on 9/1/2016, accessed on 1/3/2016

Sweid. Rami, *Education in eastern Syria: ISIS destroys future and present of students*, [online source], The New Arab, available at: https://goo.gl/tB5ewG, published on 17/6/2015, accessed on 30/7/2015

Over 60,000 students out of school in Al Raqqa... an entire generation that cannot read or write, [online source], Raqqa Is Being Slaughtered Silently, available at: http://www.raqqa-sl.com/?p=3511, published on 19/9/2016, accessed on 25/6/2016

Without pledging allegiance to the caliph... IS enlists dozens to fight in its ranks in Deir ez-Zor, [online source], The Syrian Observatory for Human Rights, available at: https://goo.gl/d9rVw5, published on 31/1/2016, accessed on 25/4/2017

Videos

24 News 2, *How does ISIS recruit children through video games?* [online source], YouTube, available at: https://goo.gl/2td5lY, published on 17/9/2015, accessed on 5/3/2016

Abas. Hsham, *IS children's training camp*, [online source], YouTube, available at: https://goo.gl/tsKfN0, published on 22/6/2015, accessed on 6/3/2016

Alkout Taqareer, *Child recruited by ISIS beheads Syrian pilot*, [online source], YouTube, available at: https://goo.gl/XRZFsN, published on 18/7/2015, accessed on 10/3/2016

Berjawi. Naim, *ISIS exploits 4-year-old British child to execute three Syrians*, [online source], YouTube, available at: https://goo.gl/U5kFTM, published on 12/2/2016, accessed on 20/2/2016

Karbala Agency News (KAN), *ISIS children trained in slaughter and killing*, [online source], YouTube, available at: https://goo.gl/VPqf9B, published on 1/10/2014, accessed on 6/3/2016

New IS release: Your rockets will not silence the smiles of children, [online source], YouTube, available at: https://goo.gl/KbJ7NZ, published on 15/10/2015, accessed on 8/3/2016

Sky News Arabia, *ISIS child kills Palestinian on the charge of spying for Israel*, [online source], YouTube, available at: https://goo.gl/0Yhaxm, published on 11/3/2015, accessed on 10/3/2016

Small speech by a caliphate cub, [online source], YouTube, available at: https://goo.gl/eRi65b, published on 28/6/2015, accessed on 12/2/2016

English Sources

Dearden. Lizzie, *ISIS training children of foreign fighters to become 'next generation' of terrorists*, [online source], Independent, available at: https://goo.gl/6l83Pm, published on 29/7/2016, accessed on 2/8/2016

Hall. John, *Our youngest martyr: ISIS boasts a jihadi fighter aged just TEN was killed as he went into battle with his father in Syria*, [online source], Mail Online, available at: https://goo.gl/gn9RNJ, published on 9/10/2014, accessed on 1/12/2014

Sengupta. Kim, *ISIS indoctrinating children to plan attacks on Big Ben, Eiffel Tower and Statue of Liberty*, [online source], INDEPENDENT, available at: https://goo.gl/ptkfWK, accessed on 25/12

Williams. Evan, *ISIS' children: Soldiers trained to kill and die*, [online source], Channel 4 News, available at: https://goo.gl/LKFKuE, published on 1/10/2015, accessed on 11/5/2015

Yoon. Sangwon, *Islamic State circulates sex slave price list*, [online source], Bloomberg Business, available at: https://goo.gl/7y6LGf, published on 4 August 2015, accessed on 15/3/2016

Wasim Raif Al Salti

Graduated from the department of Philosophy in Damascus in 2013. Wasim Raif Al Salti has taught philosophy in high schools and worked as a journalist and reporter for media outlets such as Al Arab and Assafir newspapers and Al Jadid magazine. He published several research papers such as "ISIS: Intellectual and Historical Questions" on Delta Noun website. He is currently working for Jafra Foundation for Relief and Youth Development, which works on humanitarian aid in Palestinian refugee camps in Syria.

ibidem-Verlag / *ibidem* Press
Melchiorstr. 15
70439 Stuttgart
Germany

ibidem@ibidem.eu
ibidem.eu